COMPASS IN THE EXISTENCE

COMPASS IN THE EXISTENCE

Steps to Wholeness

Daily Quotes

Margarita R. Pedrozo-Walling

Copyright © 2016 by Margarita R. Pedrozo-Walling.

Library of Congress Control Number: 2015921275
ISBN: Hardcover   978-1-5065-1090-3
          Softcover   978-1-5065-1089-7
          eBook   978-1-5065-1088-0

All rights reserved. No part of this book may be reproduced or transmitted in any form or by any means, electronic or mechanical, including photocopying, recording, or by any information storage and retrieval system, without permission in writing from the copyright owner.

Print information available on the last page.

Rev. date: 18/02/2016

To order additional copies of this book, please contact:
Palibrio
1663 Liberty Drive
Suite 200
Bloomington, IN 47403
Toll Free from the U.S.A 877.407.5847
Toll Free from Mexico 01.800.288.2243
Toll Free from Spain 900.866.949
From other International locations +1.812.671.9757
Fax: 01.812.355.1576
orders@palibrio.com
731559
www.MargaritaRosaPedrozo-Walling.com

CONTENTS

Acknowledgements vii
Prologue ix

Chapter I   January A whole of Sophistry and Vanity 1
Chapter II   February Experience as Essence 14
Chapter III March You will get what you accept. 26
Chapter IV   April The Martyrdom of Not Seeing 39
Chapter V   May The Reason to Exist is Perceptible 52
Chapter VI   June Invaluable Worth 66
Chapter VII July Folly: Limitation of the Existence 80
Chapter VIII August Wisdom or Nothing 92
Chapter IX   September Time that Happens 104
Chapter X   October Ignorance Flows from Folly 116
Chapter XI   November Charity precedes Justice 127
Chapter XII December We are Love 139

Synopsis 151
Biography 153

ACKNOWLEDGEMENTS

To my Creator for all.

To my parents who gave me life.

To life itself because of my son,

To my son for giving me strength;

And to strength that gives me growth.

In special memory of my father and to the unforgettable souls my eyes no longer see.

> ~ Do not condemn me, my soul, nor let me sink into this earthly maze. Uplift me with your essence and lead me through the path of your dawn, thus being one with the Universe. ~

PROLOGUE

It was an ordinary day following the daily routine, when a thought overflowed my mind.

Away from the world of intangible realities and hidden truths stood my sense, being stripped away from any logic as the blank sheet took flight with the pencil; while the unexpressed is being shaped clearly, it seems to be that the written word is only nebulous within the truth of human existence.

"Compass in the existence, steps to wholeness", expresses the harmonious essence of the being, which is lost in a world girdled by ego, insensitivity, greed, doubts and fears.

The text describes moments such as:

- Being wiser to understand the ravings that afflict the soul.
- Heavenly Grace as the cornerstone of wisdom and joy.
- Everything returning to the point of origin.
- Profanity and prayers being known to the divine mind.
- Worthless words being too many in an ordinary and intangible world.
- The superfluousness of life when the soul walks the path without any light.
- Foolishness as an attribute of the naïve.
- Wisdom giving harmony to the spirit and when it is shared, also brings peace.
- The common man not being able to foresee evil, until it happens.

- Lying as a restrictor of self-growth.
- The short link between ignorance and injustice.
- Love shining in the darkness.

Remembered today: A robust tree that has no roots will sooner or later fall.

Even when the ego makes you appear great, true integrity does not exist without foundation.

The ego will not give you long-term success, but only lucky breaks or vulnerable moments of recognition. Under the sunlight, the truth is not hidden.

The compass will be your fullness, taking you to new paths; where there are no more closed doors. As long as you stop to look inside your being.

CHAPTER 1

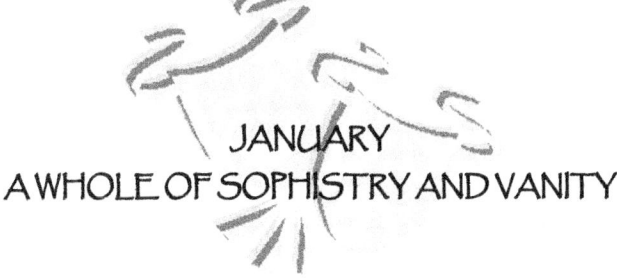

JANUARY
A WHOLE OF SOPHISTRY AND VANITY

You are the creator of yourself and of the environment around you. You have a job, call it an assignment. How painful or glorious is that which the Creator has given to man? The answer depends solely on you.

Everything is wearisome and vexing to the spirit. Thus when you labor, you manage only to get more confused, since the eye is never sated with seeing, nor the ear filled with hearing.

Have you noticed that generations come and go, or that there is a sunrise and a sunset? Have you realized that what has happened before, often occurs again? The explanation is due to the fact that there is nothing new under the sun.

Now questioning your reason, are you seeking wisdom in everything you see? In what way can the crooked be straightened and the incomplete completed? As the wind veers and swirls, it remains the wind; the river flows constantly to the sea and doesn't fill it, instead returning to its origin.

There is no remembrance of former things, nor of which of them was later.

Do you think there is understanding of what is to come?

Let yourself rise in wisdom and strengthen in its grandeur, as the wise men did before you; to understand the human senses, to be prudent, to choose what is right, (correct) and understand the ravings of the soul.

DAY 1

With material and temporal pleasures, happiness is a fallacy.

From the moment that we are born, we have two guarantees: one is happiness, and the other the departure.

Gratitude is the cornerstone of happiness, and our departure from this universe is a realization. Happiness and departure are both dimensional cognitive states revealed the same way, differing solely in the scenery.

✦ **Quote of the Day:** When your supposed happiness has vanished, its foundation was mundane.

DAY 2

This world of vanity takes us away from the silence and our inner thoughts; is living a sophistry of life with gratifications. Vanity is everything that takes us away from ourselves, baffles us and makes us feel decline; so gratification and inner peace are not found.

Our soul is calling, asking us for a conscience to see how far we are from reality. Beings made as the Creator's image.

✦ **Quote of the Day:** Adoration of vanity is hallucination to the senses; anything tangible does not last, nor is yours.

DAY 3

One cannot climb too high, pretending to own what we do not have; major error!

It is better to climb when we have knowledge of the truth without boasting of what tomorrow may bring us, if we are uninformed about it.

⊕ **Quote of the Day:** Greed does not guarantee us safety nor enlarge our existence.

DAY 4

What clogs us is what hinders, which in turn creates limitation going beyond the physical body; very far from the spiritual realm.

When we see challenges as a problem, we may not realize that the solution is also there.

⊕ **Quote of the Day:** Remember that even physical death has a spiritual solution.

DAY 5

Once man comes face to face with his own truth, he will be able to redeem his real life; the same that was overshadowed by collective or personal mistakes.

A human and spiritual criterion, centered on harmony, joy and love shall emerge.

Moral rules of men have been "boxed" following patrons, laws and doctrines which become incompatible with the conscious evolution of humanity.

⊕ **Quote of the Day:** If the right to think freely is censored, slavery follows.

DAY 6

Lack of knowledge leads to an enslaved existence; likewise, fear of "light" is similar to vanishing into the darkness.

Acquiring the absolute knowledge about existence will unfold a spiritual Compass that eventually leads to wisdom.

✥ **Quote of the Day:** When you have set out to be a voice guided by its own light, you will transcend. Similar to this, a spring breeze will let its fragrance spread around all day.

DAY 7

When we hoard we discard less; it should be the opposite. Not knowing how to despoil and remaining attached to material things gives us a false sense of normalcy, hoarding makes us feel miserable unless we do it; produces a static and negative energy which repels the positive energy flow.

Have you noticed a site full of cluttered objects abounds with dust and insects? We must apply this to the spiritual realm as well.

✥ **Quote of the Day:** Despoil to activate the flow, and remove the physical and spiritual burden as well.

DAY 8

Profane and vain words pave the way to impiety, where difficulties are manifested by unjust feelings. A righteous path is made with wise actions; with triumphs that are nourished by feelings of kindness, justice and equity.

✥ **Quote of the Day:** Listen to good advice so you can have wisdom, prudence and confidence to act; be guided by the light, like following a Compass.

DAY 9

Emotions are part of our wholeness. If we eliminate them, instability will come; which brings at the same time discontent, anguish, fear and sadness. In other words, one must learn to keep circumstances under control, so they do not affect one's inner being and its happiness.

⊕ Quote of the Day: The first step is to recognize, accept and learn how to free yourself from your own burdens, (doubts and fears) at the appropriate time, without inflicting you any harm.

DAY 10

Spiritual conformism destroys one's self esteem. We are influenced by the media and the experiences of others as well.

Being able to experience spirituality by our own emotions marks the balance between our honor and intrinsic love.

⊕ Quote of the Day: Spirituality needs not a stage, as it is manifested even during adversity.

DAY 11

Even the bravest of men come to shackles, when he is guided by his material attachments and emotional insensitivity.

Inner peace builds a solid foundation, thus faith and perseverance during troubles, give us hope for tomorrow.

⊕ Quote of the Day: A heartless man does not walk with righteousness and does not provide what is right. Without love, there is no grace from the Creator.

DAY 12

The challenges of life must be accepted with love, faith and justice. With love we accept others, as we accept ourselves. With faith we follow a spiritual path guided by providence. With justice, (truth/welfare) the Creator's justice (cosmic law) will not fall on us. The combination of these three overcomes the adversities of this world.

⊕ **Quote of the Day:** With the strength of the human being and being in harmony with the surroundings helps to perceive the imperceptible in others.

DAY 13

It is not faith that leads us to wreck, but the lack of it. Faith is the action to take, to command and to wait; but in constant spiritual movement, search for it.

As a result of the above, we have manifestations of blessings, abundance and sublimity.

⊕ **Quote of the Day:** If the link between the Creator and you is missing or broken, the process of spiritual sublimity is null.

DAY 14

Words too much preached, cannot be understood with clarity; they create endless fables and lengthy genealogies which may bring confusion, and inhibit faith in the Creator.

One must voluntarily accept wisdom and its revelations, but we must compromise if we want to understand our purpose in life.

⊕ **Quote of the Day:** If you are lacking Faith, being gracious, wise and prudent does not guarantee you a smooth way to the truth.

DAY 15

Words of blasphemy imprison the consciousness, they are also disclosed to the Creator.

We were created in his image, (divine conscience) but his word tells no lies; and God, unlike men, doesn't repent.

✠ **Quote of the Day:** God's word is eternal and truthful. Strive to stay rooted on your path, so you do not become totally helpless.

DAY 16

There is no guarantee that spiritual experiences are hassle free. To alleviate any consequences of a painful experience, we must look into the soul for revival. As the pain decreases and we apply understanding, anguish becomes strength.

It is through toil that character is formed; here a seed for humility will be born.

✠ **Quote of the Day:** You will find strength in solitude. The world around you with its hustle and bustle creates many distractions.

DAY 17

The way that leads to the truth may appear to be stormy and with many pathways, but the truth itself is simple.

No fear of uncertainty and faith keeps us on the right path. We must have the conviction that things will happen and reveal themselves at the right and beneficial moment.

✠ **Quote of the Day:** Have no fear of circumstances, rather have fear of God's words; He is the Truth. His word by divine justice has no drawbacks.

DAY 18

Acting without common sense is costly and to proceed without it is baseness; it carries consequences, as it robs the righteous man of his rightness and justifies the impious. It doesn't leave space for forgiveness.

It is like living in a world of vanity and fallacies, where false people will prevail over the truth. It leaves our wishes unfulfilled, leading to a fruitless life.

✣ **Quote of the Day:** Unfulfilled hopes will bring unrest to your conscience.

DAY 19

It has been said and is well understood that love covers all offenses and fidelity carries no secrets. Think about it, why put in risk your harmony, where there is not love, wellness and fidelity?

✣ **Quote of the Day:** Use your good judgment to act, if you do not want to break yourself.

DAY 20

Happiness is within the self; is a divine flow linked to the emotions. We should start with simple things, being content with what we possess. In the spiritual realm we never get to own any material possessions.

✣ **Quote of the Day:** Beauty without reason is like a gold ring on an ox's nose; it will have no value, serving just to pull it.

DAY 21

The mind has a psychic and sensitive mechanism that is able to capture and expand data.

It is by this mechanism that man searches for the meaning of his existence; he thus makes the mistake of encasing the spiritual concept within. Henceforth the mystic, natural, and religious phenomena are confused with the spiritual. This becomes somewhat skeptical to some and speculative to others; fallacies that are created by human unbelief.

⊕ **Quote of the Day:** We must perceive our surroundings with the soul, not with the senses.

DAY 22

The vestment doesn't make us a better human being; instead it is the spiritual concept called "Divine essence".

Our error is allowing the circumstances to take control and deform our divine essence. Why extra-sensory? Because our senses create a world of their own, and we leave behind our emotions (soul). At the same time we become distanced from our own honesty (light).

⊕ **Quote of the Day:** Lack of identity will obstruct your connection with the Creator.

DAY 23

What is the insignificance memories important, if you still remember them?

Being attached to meaningless memories, those that don't change the life for good and even may become a trap way; turning into a mega problem when we focus on the past, attracting their negative energy just by thinking about them.

"Bad moments" (a term imposed by the individual or society itself) don't exist; instead there are opportunities to choose.

✦ **Quote of the Day:** No matter what your decision might be, reaching dawn (your light) will be even harder if you are engrossed in the sundown (darkness).

DAY 24

Do not that lead to straight paths, good formation and gratification are:

Do not betray someone's trust.

Do not be an agent to ignite quarrels.

Do not covet someone's possessions.

Do not choose the easy path.

Do not be a miser.

✦ **Quote of the Day:** If you act with intelligence and satisfy your inner search, all light and wisdom will be in your path, because you have honored yourself and others.

DAY 25

When the individual will it is given to vanity (fallacy) and what others want, strength is weakened and self-dishonor is born. A state of frenzy gives way to error, as it falters without correction in the attempt at life that may remain.

✦ **Quote of the Day:** No regret is more deafening than an empty old age; when all that surrounds is but a sea of debris and unfulfilled dreams.

DAY 26

Difficulties are not what torment men; difficulties already have a solution, and they should be accepted.

What truly ails men are unfulfilled hopes, as they put the strongest men in shackles.

It is better to walk the road full of darts than to walk the easy path that becomes a way without return.

⊕ **Quote of the Day:** Lust and vanity are two material things that go together and which contradict with the spiritual state.

DAY 27

The truth of existence is simple and is based on the connection that exists between humility, kindness and morality. This connection has a spiritual base and it has to do with our relationship with God's creation.

The lack of this knowledge leads to a selfish life full of obstacles.

⊕ **Quote of the Day:** This is about understanding and strengthening the relationship between Creator Vis a Vis men and men Vis a Vis creation. Being made in His image means, we have a divine consciousness and we are able to share.

DAY 28

Acting with a spiritual conviction means, we practice sharing as a life style. Doing so brings satisfaction as well and the self is in harmony with the surroundings. Then, within the whole cosmos, where truth and light are related and hence negativity is repelled; so that the soul (being attached to the self) is following a divine Compass.

✠ **Quote of the Day:** Everything is created. Our purpose is to discover and relate with the whole in collective harmony, discarding any evidence of egotism.

DAY 29

"Personal achievement" means indeed personal.

When we live in a world of confusion, it will be reflected on the spiritual realm as well.

A material loss may be replaced, but a spiritual loss can last forever. That is why we should be concerned about the spiritual first.

✠ **Quote of the Day:** We should not equate spiritual time with physical time. Spiritual time relates to eternity, physical time passes each second; spiritual time is in constant and evaluative transformation, physical time destroys the matter around it, when not in harmony with the surroundings.

DAY 30

The truth was existing before the lie.

There is a truth beneath every lie. There is no lie (vanity: falsehood and illusion to the senses) in the spiritual realm, all is perceived trough the Soul, which makes no mistakes. In the material realm all is perceived trough the senses, which are limited and prone to err, producing fallacies.

✠ **Quote of the Day:** Compass is the balance of those realms. Even if you are wise and prudent in your acts, there is not guaranteed path without infelicities and tumbling blocks, (acts of others or your own) especially if your spirituality is false.

DAY 31

A righteous man, in the full meaning of the word, is the one who acts with goodness for all and to all; with no space for lies; he will always walk with rectitude and integrity.

Just advice is always welcome, even if it is to rebuke; bringing comfort to the soul and strengthening the physical will.

✠ **Quote of the Day:** With understanding and prudence, the road is lighter and your soul is free. Thus your labor prospers, and there will be no obstacles to happiness, the opposite road leads just to bitterness.

CHAPTER II

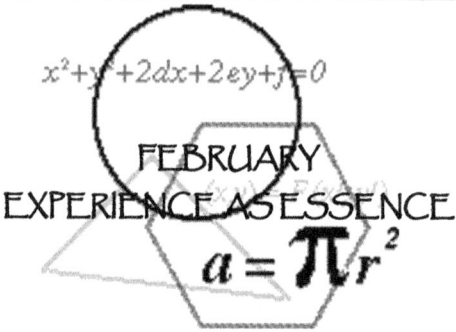

FEBRUARY
EXPERIENCE AS ESSENCE

All material things and pleasures are unreal to our divine essence, as they are false in the spiritual realm. Do material goods make us happy? Do they prove to be of service to our soul as well? What good is the daily toil for ones who are far from practicing wisdom in the affairs of the soul, as they do not refrain from folly?

Who said that one needs to walk away from wisdom in order to live in harmony with the surroundings?

If we pay close attention to the definition of wisdom and to the concept of foolishness; we see that affliction to the spirit doesn't bring joy to one's soul, but foolishness and wisdom's demised. On the other hand, people who see with understanding will be in the realm of learned experience and thus will not be overwhelmed by delirium.

Why do you have to despise life and everything accomplished? Do not! It is experience that is earned as part of the search, understanding and spiritual uplifting.

You should not let your reason get lost for the time that has been wasted on that daily inane vanity.

It is never too late to find the grace of the Creator, which belongs to us by design. It would be eternal martyrdom to depart from this world without having His grace. We then allow our soul to rejoice in its work (experiences) so that the path is a caring one; in so far as we take care of ourselves, we are filled with heavenly grace which is the basis of wisdom and harmonious joy (personal and collective).

When we please the Creator, everything works out well without much effort.

DAY 1

Wisdom is the best gift we can give to ourselves. Let's begin to lay the basis for it.

- Moving away from folly (ignorance).
- Accepting self-correction and criticism as well (rectitude).
- Giving love and gratitude (justice).
- Rejecting perdition (dishonor) or any spiritual turpitude (confusion).

⊕ **Quote of the Day:** Foolishness, lack of wisdom, is a constant anxiety that you will carry along. Do not be resistant to self-growth.

DAY 2

Fairness and its benefits.

- There are no errors of karma.
- Knowing the truth helps build good behavior.
- A diligent character will never beg.
- The path will be blessed even when it turns into tribulation time for others.
- Having prudence in speech is like giving good advice during times of confusion.

✦ **Quote of the Day:** An honest man is always well received and remembered.

DAY 3

Being unfair and its implications.

- Errors come from Karma, eternal transcendental suffering.
- Lack of understanding creates a wicked being.
- A negligent character creates a violent, lazy being.
- The road then will be one of confusion, brokenness and destruction.
- One's foolish words then become slander and lies about others.

✦ **Quote of the Day:** When your soul is empty, peace, wisdom and understanding will not manifest.

DAY 4

Arrogance and anger are signs of someone wicked, who in his own ignorance brings shame to himself, and therefore is not worthy of trust. Believing in him is a lost cause.

✦ **Quote of the Day:** When you are wise enough to ignore an offense, silence will bring gratification rather than torment.

DAY 5

Do not confuse "abundant intelligence" with "wisdom". Have you ever seen a man who is opulent and wise as well?

Intelligence may bring you riches but will not make you humble, might take you as well by beautiful roads, but crooked. May fill you with prestige as well, but the later will also be forgotten when you fall. Intelligence becomes a torment when spiritual instruction is not observed.

⊕ **Quote of the Day:** Thus intelligence can become your reason's enemy but wisdom will take you to the reason.

DAY 6

When the path to spirituality disquiets us, urging us to seek more answers there is no reason to come to a halt. It will indeed be the correct way.

When the spiritual life becomes routine it puts limits to existence and becomes a barrier to finding its own truth. Conformism leads to a stagnant life even when it feels easygoing.

In the search for daily changes, there are countless tangible possibilities in a countless space of light. Spirituality is limitless joy.

⊕ **Quote of the Day:** Unaccepted experiences don't bring satisfaction; emptiness will follow.

DAY 7

When the surroundings are unsettling, it is not a good idea to stay. The right approach will be to observe and let go, otherwise, you'll fall and badness take over.

Only the laws of good will keep you, and only the truth will exalt you.

Setting obstacles against achievement is like the result of a choice, which is not based on reason; is the effect and not the cause.

When all actions taken are harmonious and for a good cause, they will bring only more light and perfection, (paths of righteousness) while there is a happy attitude.

✧ **Quote of the Day:** Depart from criticism, doubt and perversity, they are the basis for your own stumbling. Your step should always be for a better future.

DAY 8

Disparagement will condemn you. When you act with apathy, you are being negligent with the surroundings and blessings that have been given to you; therefore you are practicing a caged form of hatred. Love, peace, and harmony are missing as a result of these self-destructive thoughts; collective despair as well as wickedness and egotism take their place, impetuous arrogance prevails; in this context the most vulnerable will fall and will be like "the walking dead".

✧ **Quote of the Day:** Being able to accept your reality (good) on a daily basis means you are being honest within, loving yourself and to others.

DAY 9

The next time we beg for mercy, we must remember how merciful we have been with others, in order to be attended by the Creator. It could happen that today by any luck we are granted some comfort. For how much longer are we going to be under that grace?

✧ **Quote of the Day:** One must discard a haughty and oppressive character in order to see the hope (soul wishes) become a real miracle on our lives.

DAY 10

Wordiness is a threat to proactivity. If you want to be heard and affirmed (assured,) you must walk in understanding.

How do you transmit your thoughts if you don't understand yourself?

Without any understanding your words and actions become absurd; as a result your search will only bring about confusion; you must be prepared.

How do we take the first step? Humility will help us leave behind iniquity and spiritual poverty.

⊕ **Quote of the Day:** Feel the need to seek the truth; leaving behind the love for the mirage of the material world. The correct word is like a blessing.

DAY 11

Are difficulties a part of our daily lives? It could be so, but even when we allow it to be; the solution may be closer than we think. There is a Compass in taking a direct approach towards them rather than avoiding them; by doing this, we can have conscious growth and avoid affliction of the spirit.

⊕ **Quote of the Day:** The joy of your soul is the result of an inwardly manifested truth, even during dark and vile days.

DAY 12

Is there anything unseen behind a new dawn? No! It is here where lies fade and truth gets revealed. Desperation does not help at all, unless we seek for lasting pity.

When we are alert, we measure our steps against evil; as every false step would cause us eternal unrest (confusion).

⊕ **Quote of the Day:** Folly is arrogance and certainty is wisdom. We must correct with prudence and listen with understanding.

DAY 13

There is always truth in the good. When truth is rejected we are foolish; we use words without any basis, we have unworthy feelings, and dishonor becomes part of our daily lives. There is a need to be generous with friends and the needy as well.

Make sure you act with prudence, as haste is not a good counselor for your walk. Discard anger, it is a character's foul.

⊕ **Quote of the Day:** There is no good in inequality and a prudent person does not boast of his own kindness.

DAY 14

There are material and spiritual riches. Material riches (vanity) do not make your light shine. Spiritual riches do feed your light; material ones destroy and spiritual ones edify; material ones feed on hatred and envy as well, while spiritual ones thrive with compassion and sharing.

⊕ **Quote of the Day:** Riches intended to acquire wickedness will not contribute to a solid foundation to anyone.

DAY 15

The rewind button allows us to go back when using digital devices. We must take the time to make corrections at ones; trying to fix mistakes later may not yield the same result.

When we do not apply intelligence to constructive activities (to get rid of mental inertia) we then fall into a void where harmonious judgment is transformed up to the point of negative bewilderment, without any advance.

✦ **Quote of the Day:** Using reasonable thinking step by step, you will find the "why" of your existence.

DAY 16

Acting with prudence will avert suffering and other people's blasphemies will be no threat to us. Being prudent sets the foundation of the just and the diligent, where there is no room for anger.

✦ **Quote of the Day:** You will eat from the fruit of your mouth.

DAY 17

Where wisdom abides there is no arrogance, but prudence. Prudence is manifested by the spoken word, thus strengthening one's essence.

✦ **Quote of the Day:** To be able to listen to advice and to understand the truth, means you will acquire satisfaction and peace during maturity.

DAY 18

Understanding cannot be acquired through riches; the riches will not guarantee a prosperous heritage.

The difference between a wise man and a fool with riches, is that understanding builds men of good and knowledge, able to love the truth in them.

✦ **Quote of the Day:** Repressions are good for the understanding.

DAY 19

The person who practices common sense will not be a victim of furor. Any advice derived from furor will disrupt the wisdom.

✦ **Quote of the Day:** Understanding will help us reach to the depths of any advice received.

DAY 20

A fulfilled life during middle age is the result of practicing love and compassion in the early days. A noble attitude will bring glory, truth and a living force.

✦ **Quote of the Day:** You will receive according to your deeds.

DAY 21

Acting without common sense or good reasons, will keep you separated from truth and goodness. One despises life and also the words expressed are perverted, iniquitous, evil, critical and condemned. A perverted man will always be despised.

✦ **Quote of the Day:** There will be light and perfection coming your way when you act with wisdom toward material things, as well, when you observe a spiritual discipline, you will bring solace to your soul.

DAY 22

When the pursuit of glory is corrupted with greed, it will bring misfortune. The soul will feed from left overs; perhaps the future appears bright but the outcome is not in our hands.

✦ **Quote of the Day:** Action's reason is not what feeds the soul.

DAY 23

Honesty begins with you. The first step, is to accept mistakes and faults that plague the conscience. Second step, we must look for revival and cleansing of our soul. Third step, after completing steps one and two, we must not forget the spiritual being within us.

⊕ **Quote of the Day:** Avoid being a victim of your own deceit.

DAY 24

One of man's transcendental errors is satiety.

When we are not satisfied with having in excess, we lose our sense of value, and at the same time end up taking things for granted. The Compass will remind us how important it is to share; whatever we have or don't have. By doing so, we will learn to regain from the lost.

⊕ **Quote of the Day:** In one's spiritual way (life) there is no satiety, but "growth".

DAY 25

It is in this material world where the self is more insecure, making it easy to fall into injustice and sorrows, creating a constant emptiness in humanity. Instead, a spiritual life bring security. Why? Justice is what makes us perfect in front the Creator.

Peace, which gives us internal happiness, (self-satisfaction) is only achieved with quietude (patience) of conscience. Thus is activated the perception that our actions harmonize with success.

✦ **Quote of the Day:** Do not snub out your spirit but lull it, so that you can feel where its force is leading you.

DAY 26

The folly of an adult is not the same as the prank of a child.

Fools despise even their friends; their words are not to be trusted. The difference between an adult and a child who are both foolish, is that the adult envies due to his lack of truth and the child due to his age.

✦ **Quote of the Day:** An adult with envy is like a virus active deep within the bone. The years lived should result in better sense.

DAY 27

Words can work magic. Kind words can soothe anger, sincere words will heal misfortune, and when they are uttered with conscience (truth), they will open a path to light. Words spoken with iniquity will be like a torment to others.

✦ **Quote of the Day:** There is no blasphemy in righteous words.

DAY 28

"If you don't listen to good advice, you may never get older". Old age, likewise, solace acquired through the knowledge of the truth and accomplished hopes. This may happen after we accept with prudence and humility the wise advice we are given; otherwise we live in constant scorn that ages the self in its foundations (essence).

✦ **Quote of the Day:** One should feed the spiritual self in order to beautify old age.

DAY 29

Conscious knowledge enables men to build a bridge between the individual and the universal life.

The common error is the one which denies our universal nature. Human beings have the ability to convert experiences into conscious acts which constantly evolve.

All of our actions and habits have a domino effect; we move a piece and everything takes place for better or worse.

⊕ **Quote of the Day:** If a negative circumstance already took place, do not try to change it, you shall be the one who must modify, adapt and accept it with love.

CHAPTER III

MARCH
YOU WILL GET WHAT YOU ACCEPT.

There is a time for everything, for what is intended and for what is desired; therefore eagerness, bewilderment and folly should have no place in a harmonious daily life. Let's start a new beginning by:

- Understanding and accepting the truth of the Creator in each being.
- Learning to have joy in everything we do.
- Find the daily balance between happiness and good.
- Being able to accept the clock's precision; every event has its appointed time.
- Being able to understand that all created life is everlasting; as there is no ending with a perfect balance.
- Being able to understand that the past is past and the future is also past. Always the past can be restored.
- Being able to accept that we are alike. We all share the same success and the same air as well.
- Being able to understand that we go back to the point of origin.
- Being able to understand that the beginning and the end are always transformed and they both return.
- Being able to understand that not all that surround us build us; we see the difference when we trust in the truth.

There should be no eagerness to create sophistry (vanity, illusions and imperceptible moments) since the result is product of the emptiness of the self. If we think that after we depart from this world we will be able to see the unfinished works we left behind, we are far from the truth.

DAY 1

Happiness without doubt is the basis of good living, and misfortune shadows existence. Therefore, our actions, as well as our words can make a difference between happiness and misery, as they also have the power of life and death.

Actions that are perpetrated with wickedness will cause disputes and be a barrier to other people's happiness. Nonsense and empty words, create a storm over others.

⊕ **Quote of the Day:** When your words or actions are maliciously intended towards others, you are carving your own misfortune.

DAY 2

The difference between a loser and a successful entrepreneur is that the loser lives encased in his thoughts, while the successful one lives up to every challenge.

Challenges, however small or big they may be, must be confronted so they do not become a stumbling block along the way.

⊕ **Quote of the Day:** Challenges must be taken; if we avoid them they become obstacles on your path of light.

DAY 3

Avoiding corrections at the due time is equal to supporting a low self-esteem.

There is hope with correction; and a strong character as well. When there is low self-esteem, the self is liable to sell even its own conscience. A strong character leaves no room for despondency or discouragement, and no room for fear. A weak character abounds with shame and foolishness, and clings to a self-destructive fear.

✦ **Quote of the Day:** Your physical actions will be harmonious and full if they are fueled by the interior essence.

DAY 4

To ignore an offense will help us avoid a meaningless fight.

The fatuous man insults due to ignorance, disgrace, and egoistic pleasure; he does so because he is unable to recognize that he is beneath the one he is trying to insult.

Good relationships are established when we accept our faults and we are discrete with other people's faults.

✦ **Quote of the Day:** Angry outbursts are bonds of bitterness for the soul.

DAY 5

The difference between hunger due to laziness and hunger due to ignorance, is that the lazy one doesn't search for opportunities, while the ignorant one fails to understand that there is an opportunity open for him.

✦ **Quote of the Day:** If you live with haste, you become tedious. If you are well satisfied, you will sleep in oblivion.

DAY 6

Wealth with avarice, will bring enemies and servants. Wealth is as irrational as poverty which falls into rejection and loneliness;

to think that such a man will be strengthened and his soul saved.

✠ **Quote of the Day:** Haughtiness, pride and wickedness will lead to perdition for a reason.

DAY 7

Delight can give you material privileges, but will never fill your spiritual need. The paths to step in truth are open; walking on them will lead you to spiritual harmony. Spiritual harmony will give you comfort, unlike satisfying material needs.

✠ **Quote of the Day:** When the road seems hard, keep hope; it will never allow you to compromise your truth.

DAY 8

There are two available choices to make: wisdom and pride.

Wisdom:

- Is observed with understanding.
- Is constructive till the last day.
- Is part of the truth.
- Gives assurance.
- Does not yield to pride.
- Pays attention to all, including offenses.

Pride:

- Look without understanding.
- Destroys till the last day.
- Deforms the truth.
- Acts without certainty.
- The haughty believes he is wise.
- Pride insults without listening

✦ **Quote of the Day:** Prudence affirms, understanding will sustain you, and wisdom will reinforce you as a being of "light" (divine).

DAY 9

"Demanding an eye for an eye is like having thorns in the hand or having poison in the spoken word."

If we only knew that whoever does evil is wronging himself more than the person he intends to harm, because this acting without reasons represses the rights of others. It is like living with a fainted spirit.

✦ **Quote of the Day:** Those who refuse to accept their reality, vent their anger on others and live a restless life.

DAY 10

There is no point in correcting the unwise, as they will never understand the spoken word. You must answer to the fool according to his folly if you don't want to become his enemy.

It is sad for the ones who deceive themselves; as in reality they are just empty vessels.

✦ **Quote of the Day:** Being wise is the same as being integral, prudent and fair. It is having a whole of spirituality.

DAY 11

A good start does not necessarily end that way, therefore we must never put our guard down.

When we walk in confusion, there is no certainty as to where our path may lead us.

Let us think about the cause and effect of which road to take; let's connect with all that is within us, thus eliminating our own selfish limitations.

✠ **Quote of the Day:** Do not put restraints on your wisdom, and rather let it fly.

DAY 12

"Running with patience" sounds contradictory!

It refers to quickening itself with knowledge in a gentle manner, but being firm, at the same time applying Love and Peace. Is the act of shedding the irrational will in order to make proper choices; in such a plan there is no room for the words "dishonor" and "profanity".

✠ **Quote of the Day:** A calamity cannot be a bad thing when it is submitted to the Creator's will in prayer.

DAY 13

Without doubt, miracles do manifest where both human and natural prospects fail; or when the expected result is far from being revealed by the senses.

✠ **Quote of the Day:** "Faith" is an act of will, to believe is an act of reason and trust is an emotional act, but without emotions there is no faith.

DAY 14

Without a doubt, an unrestrained tongue can damage the reason. When there is much talk, the lie will have its boom, giving room for disgrace. It is easy to understand that prudence is the basis of understanding; on the other hand, impiety sets the stage for disparagement.

Speaking of spirituality's path we understand that easy words and false testimony are a blasphemy to the soul. Words uttered with conscience will bring rejoicing.

Why should we partake of a deceitful tongue, which runs around in gossip, as it uncovers secrets?

⊕ **Quote of the Day:** A tongue that feeds from remnants will also be bereft.

DAY 15

Is the time our best or worst enemy?

That category was invented by men and his conduct. Time is just a passing moment for which we are accountable and such has no return; henceforth the proverb, "Do not leave for tomorrow what you can do today"; is valid.

Which is the true essence? Not letting your opportunity in life pass you by, you must do your duty today.

Time changes and transforms any rational being, and destroy an irrational one.

⊕ **Quote of the Day:** Time can become your own barrier when there is no consciousness of your act. There is no lost time, rather underutilized time.

DAY 16

Lack of respect sets the ground for shame; causing with it the fall to a low level of spirituality.

Dishonoring parents will bring dark trails, as will honoring those who proceed with pride and wickedness.

✥ **Quote of the Day:** A secret fault will bring shame when it is uncovered.

DAY 17

When has it ever been confirmed that a lie has been a good mediator?

It would be like saying that summer is like snow and the rain is like drought.

There is a misunderstanding as to white lies; as there is no such thing as a white lie or a gossip being small.

A pious lie will equally bring chaos, taking the slightest misunderstanding to a maximum conflict. Both are as damaging as the wicked act of thinking iniquity.

A conflict growing stronger may cause the fall of a nation.

The liar and the impious are equally guilty, like the one who, guided by ignorance, lives in a constant lie.

✥ **Quote of the Day:** Lying is like a boomerang which returns with a curse; gossiping otherwise is like a sweet snack with harmful effect on one's health.

DAY 18

What is the use of a fake path of righteousness when selfishness is at hand with the ego and impiety? As a result there are no just actions, much less compassion.

That state of evil living, is the result of a rebuke that wasn't given or wasn't accepted, and even less understood.

✦ **Quote of the Day:** One must accept the clamor and benevolent advice of others, if you want to be heard of and thus be a role model.

DAY 19

Have you ever wondered, how useful are words if they cannot be understood or give you advice?

Lying words reach the heart, flattering words cause damage, and words of hatred show no mercy. All of them, sooner or later, will reveal our own misery to others.

✦ **Quote of the Day:** Words of blasphemy and deceit will not only cause damage to the already injured.

DAY 20

There is a misleading furor with wickedness, insolence, greed and bragging.

A state of falsehood and greed may allow us to take advantage of others; however the scorning will not last.

Not being confirmed in truth will convert us into hated human beings who proclaim their greatness over and over again, but with an anguished soul.

Impiety is a daily bread, boasting in a false life and freedom; not realizing that we are like a summer night and the dry wind.

✦ **Quote of the Day:** Do not rush into things, that you do not know how to end.

DAY 21

There is a power in silence, the same force that moves us after a storm, the unexpected force that shakes the heart, which helps us overcome difficulty as we patiently wait.

✢ **Quote of the Day:** Listen to your spirit in stillness; recognize and activate the freedom that harmonizes with your soul.

DAY 22

A wise man does not walk a path of rebellion.

The evildoer will not hurt him; and the simplicity of others will not disturb him.

Unlike the wicked, who understand only conflict, the wise man recognizes and avoids it, thus living in constant harmony with his surroundings.

✢ **Quote of the Day:** A genuine crown through generations will be acquired with understanding.

DAY 23

Adversity leads to two results: One is the destruction of the material and the other edification of the character. This character must be forged by the purity of the Spirit.

Bitterness is the sign that there is a reality that needs to be accepted, and emotional needs that need to be addressed. Bitterness leads to spiritual poverty.

✢ **Quote of the Day:** When you recognize what leads you to adversity (negativity) and you transform it, you will be strengthened and your spirit will be purified, it will be overwhelmed by joy and your soul will be in Compass with the surroundings.

DAY 24

The hopes placed on the iniquitous or wicked, are lost hopes. True hopes are the ones that are entrusted to the Creator's will.

A wish that is not revealed will be lost, resulting in emptiness and darkness of the self.

Lack of passion and a fragile spiritual state will cause one to lose the gifts given.

⊕ **Quote of the Day:** If you want to be Happy, believe in Hope and do not stop wishing.

DAY 25

Do not think about it too much, just accept it: "Pain can turn into good"

When we accept and understand the reason for pain, fears, sadness, trauma and suffering; they go away.

The Compass will help you understand that pain was destined for you, to make you stronger, and to heal you; at the same time it will correct you from errors and fears and keep you from darkness.

⊕ **Quote of the Day:** Unconscious pain will keep you away from your spiritual conscience; and from the path of light as well.

DAY 26

Interior growth is what makes us unique; doing it with humility will give us courage.

✣ **Quote of the Day:** When you rush to be ready before your time, you will be like a small ripe fruit and your essence will not be appreciated.

DAY 27

We are like three in one; everything depends on who we want to become in this world.
- Active people never cease to learn, and are ready to confront the daily challenges.
- Passive people will follow other people's steps and do not care about challenge.
- Neutral people see life passing by as they do not understand the meaning of a new day.

✣ **Quote of the Day:** A strong spirit is one who understands the meaning of "Life"

DAY 28

The only work that is permanent day and night, is not rewarded and will cause one to be blessed, is at everyone's reach. Are you ready? It is within you, it is spiritual work.

The requirement is to walk not in darkness, and to be able to change and to walk extra miles.

✣ **Quote of the Day:** The internal change that will guide you to the light, (encounter with the Creator) will happen, if there is a high level of consciousness and knowledge; trusting the Creator is a reciprocal agreement.

DAY 29

Darkness and traps will always be encountered on the way; however the real problem, as well as the bad part, is to fall into them, leaving good behind.

When we despise our surroundings and don't learn from what is good, we get confused; it is like trying to turn the light off with the inane trust that there will be dawn.

✥ **Quote of the Day:** If you want to grow stronger in your spirit, you must have to get over what bothers you.

Day 30

Negative patterns are part of our evolution. How?

When we recognize them, we leave behind our hatred and we look to complement each other in the search for what makes us happy. We stop being invalids and we change into "complete souls".

✥ **Quote of the Day:** Do not complain about life's difficulties, for they are part of your spiritual existence; if you have them, you will be able to transform yourself to do good deeds. You ought to worry if you don't have any!

DAY 31

How important we must be for the Creator if days convert into nights and nights into days; all goes and comes with them.

It tells us every moment that nothing is permanent, but simply what is experienced with conscience.

The Compass is to live with the light and with assurance that happiness, if quite hard to achieve, is not impossible at all.

✥ **Quote of the Day:** Happiness is not related to materiality. Spirituality will fill you with greatness. Everything is at your fingertips, if you wish!

CHAPTER IV

APRIL
THE MARTYRDOM OF NOT SEEING

Bad actions, even though they may only result from ignorance, have consequences; ignorance is not a shield.

When discussing bad actions, we refer to everything that ails the spirit including vanity, envy, oppression, sadness and evil deeds.

When we live in foolishness (ignorance), we fall into an illusion that we drag with us into old age. We must remember that even the wealthy and learned can be foolish. Folly is ignorance of truth and spirituality, especially if we ignore how to govern ourselves, not others.

We are deluded whenever we place our trust in a fool who talks a lot and lacks good deeds!

Losers we are, when we justify our mistakes by ignorance, forgetting that our blasphemies, like our prayers are heard and the responses to them will also fall.

DAY 1

There is no excuse for anyone who justifies evil; he and the evildoer, both fall equally low.

The damage will be to such an extent that one's brokenness will be unavoidable; when one is complicit in evil, the expression of the soul is hidden. The face will always express insensitivity.

✠ **Quote of the Day:** Infamy, anger, and grudges can never be justified; they bring thorns to your home and surrounding.

DAY 2

When a time of distress seems confusing, we must avoid three false steps so the rebellious do not rejoice over our affliction.
- Let ourselves be consumed by wrath
- Lay our hopes in the hands of others.
- Allow foolishness to be our advisor.

These steps are like wood to feed fire, as they are the result of our own fears.

✠ **Quote of the Day:** Wrath, envy and fury are as heavy as a stone, and they may blind you like sand in the eyes.

DAY 3

Persons are tested by what they proclaim. Why do you praise yourself?

We must understand that truth is the only thing which will not remove us from our own throne.

✠ **Quote of the Day:** Do not blow your nose too hard if you are afraid of blood.

DAY 4

Abhorring our surroundings will keep a world of opportunities away from us.

Actions from a confused mind, will cause us to be feed on bitterness and to despise the honey that is truth; meanwhile dissatisfaction will abound.

When we live in impiety, we are flattering our own neighbor and hiding our hands from our own parents.

To hide the damage is like trying to hold the air with one's hand.

✦ **Quote of the Day:** To give is to receive and to deny is to accept lack.

DAY 5

The competition that helps you grow is the one you wage on your own; is the art of knowing how to live; be better than your "ego".

We are not alone; there will always be somebody working with us toward our aspirations or fighting against them.

The advantage of a conscious being is that he can keep steadily on; learning what is convenient and rejecting what is not.

✦ **Quote of the Day:** The fulfillment of becoming a harmonious being may be complicated, but is not impossible.

DAY 6

Life's priority must be centered within our own sincerity; doing what is in harmony with the self, the truth.

Love is the center of everything, however there are people who will not accept us; that is no reason to get discouraged. Appreciation must become for us a secondary interest. Let's focus on accepting ourselves as our first priority; the rest will fall into place at the proper time.

⊕ **Quote of the Day:** Life's trials are easier to take if you know with certainty that everything will be okay at the end of a process. It will be as it is meant to be.

DAY 7

Advice that is well received is like fresh ointment. Once the correction is accepted and the lesson learned, peace and joy will follow.

When we insist on our foolishness, we may stumble into a bickering path; our peaceful righteousness is replaced by misleading fury, as we become shameful beings prone to act out hatred and abominations. Fury is lethal to the soul, and a mockery to fullness.

⊕ **Quote of the Day:** A friend who is close is worth more than a brother who is far.

DAY 8

Antonyms of success, "never and already: I will never get there, I have already succeeded."

The difference between extended success and a short lived one, lies recognizing that we are the channel for a manifestation that will serve to be of inspiration to others, rather than to our own irrational ego.

⊕ **Quote of the Day:** Ego is the antonym of happiness, and the synonym of frustration.

DAY 9

There is no room to doubt the phrase: "Strive if you want to progress"!

There is another phrase as valuable and good as the previous one: "The right path in life focuses on listening, giving and receiving."

✠ **Quote of the Day:** Life is the same, but you are the one that changes. Strive to use and your strength for good; maximum extreme.

DAY 10

We do not fear our responsibilities when they become a compromise; fear is then the basis of failure. Obligations are there, but we are capable of coping with them.

Being filled with easy realizations will bring emptiness and disappointment.

✠ **Quote of the Day:** Recognizing the importance of our good actions and the surroundings as well, you are ready for progressive change.

DAY 11

Words have a profound meaning, when they are listened to with conscience without any contempt or condition. Words without love have a negative effect, like a shockwave.

✠ **Quote of the Day:** An angry word feeds not the soul, but the ego.

DAY 12

Worries can reach such extremes that they can keep us away from happiness and even our own reason. That is what happens when we worry about what others think about us.

⊕ **Quote of the Day:** The self-destructive instinct and the senses are not in control when happiness is far from being pleasant.

DAY 13

Life has a divine and a human time.

With the divine time, one is eternal and able to be reborn daily, here the soul control the senses. ith the human time, one is mortalal, able to be reborn dayliol when happiness is far being pleasant.With the human time, one is mortal and dies every day; here the reason controls the senses. When we unite theme, we become a conscious human being.

⊕ **Quote of the Day:** When we understand the reason for that unification, we achieve a high degree of wisdom, along with the ability to change our surroundings.

DAY 14

Maybe we can say, on many occasions, which something of the same sort can heal us and also let us see the truth.

To recover from a snake bite, one needs an antidote from the same venom.

To overcome fear, you need to cope with it with more fear; fearing about where you go, if you can't confront your frustrations and limitations, or resolve the chaos. The key is to doubt that this fear, is not a fear.

Fear is empty, and the acceptation of such is plentitude; which will weaken fear at the end.

⊕ **Quote of the Day:** Strength is within you, if you wish it.

DAY 15

Wishes and yearning in our lives are like a boomerang, if we launch it early, hoping, it will return just in time to our lives.

When the rules of the game are known, the moves are monitored in constant evolution. You are the starting point, with an unpredictable turn of events.

⊕ **Quote of the Day:** Your destiny is the result of your actions, which are deployed like a boomerang; what goes around comes around.

DAY 16

How do we know that we walk in the right direction?

When it is not discovered yet; it is one that will surprise you with new challenges and changes for the better. One which is not a conditioned routine, giving us a state of freedom and prosperity.

⊕ **Quote of the Day:** We must appreciate the new day as if it were the first one to discover; taking solace in it, as if it were your last day.

DAY 17

Positive actions become useless if negative patterns are not changed.

Judging and lack of compassion are part of human nature. The soul tends to lead us towards unconditional service.

To be oblivious to other people's pain will cause us emotional and spiritual entrapment; it acts as an antagonist to prosperity, and a life full of light.

⊕ **Quote of the Day:** Even when we are the Creator's essence, we are far away to be like Him. Do not judge.

DAY 18

Physical vision is limited, spiritual vision is infinite. Physical vision is perceived by the senses and the spiritual one is transcended by the soul.

There is a barrier between both visions, created by the ego and with it, a false existence which hides the truth.

Intellect brings you closer to reality; spirituality brings you closer to the truth; the combination of the two, leads to wisdom.

⊕ **Quote of the Day:** Not all that is real is truth; but truth will be always real.

DAY 19

Whenever we declare that there is nothing good in life for us, we make it happen by failing to keep our emotions under control, and by rejecting spirituality.

By controlling our negative energy, we use our time in the search of a positive change. Controlling those emotions opposed to what we believe, is not a limitation, but rather a mapped path for spiritual growth.

Spirituality should not produce shame; if it happens, we move away from an "I am" and we engage in an "I am like".

✥ **Quote of the Day:** Spirituality will make you unique within a whole.

DAY 20

Our senses are earthly sensory perceptions, but not our spiritual connection.

When we are above the senses, soul vibrations will manifest and everything around us will

have a different picture, being not far from the truth.

✥ **Quote of the Day:** Looking back after knowing the truth will cause dishonor to your soul.

DAY 21

When we proclaim our good deeds, we are showing contempt for nobility. Contempt, unlike love, cannot be hidden in the heart.

With truth and honesty, the purity of our emotions will be revealed as well as actions shared.

✥ **Quote of the Day:** Rejection is dissatisfaction's cornerstone, gratefulness is the cornerstone for fulfillment. Contempt is the basis for your own dissatisfaction, appreciation is the basis for realization

DAY 22

If only we learned to be like the hands on the clock, we would notice that every second ends and each one brings something new.

Everything is in constant change and if we want to be part of that harmony and evolution, we must understand creation as a whole in a synchronized movement, which sets each difference for good, as long as our consciousness is in the TIC-TAC: Take It, Change – Take Action, Control

✢ **Quote of the Day:** You are an individual with collective roots, so your actions will have a domino effect when they are wrong, or illumination when they are correct.

DAY 23

What will become of those who believing they are integral, but are turbid or the ones who are a curse to their parents instead of a blessing?

What will happen to the ones whose selfish egos do not let them react with compassion and, as they walk, step on and crush the poor?

No great works can be achieved -much less something worthy- unless a blood price is paid.

✢ **Quote of the Day:** Your reasons are based on your self-righteousness.

DAY 24

There are events and actions in life that are hidden and leave no trace, like the bird's flight through the air. Our actions leave a trace. The purpose of our existence is to win most of them.

✢ **Quote of the Day:** Do not fear your reflection in the mirror, but fear the reflection of your actions on the cosmic mirror of Living.

DAY 25

Joy brings harmony to the soul, and will not allow doubt or disappointment.

Celestial energy makes you untouchable, however sadness strips all objects of their charm; it carries the prospect of a future in darkness, depriving the soul of its aspirations.

Sadness produces a chain of negative power, producing in us something like a mental paralysis.

⊕ **Quote of the Day:** Joy gives you wings and melancholy gives you heavy feet.

DAY 26

You will not reap passionfruit if you plant limes. The desired fruition takes longer than expected. The process can be dilatory and frustrating, when we crave more for our own satisfaction.

The Compass of an abundant harvest is on sowing regardless of time, place or circumstance; in other words, without expecting anything in return.

⊕ **Quote of the Day:** Sowing with love will make you reap beyond earthly gratification.

DAY 27

Problems without relevance, past or imaginary...What is their significance in our world?

Here is the Compass with which to cope: Fix them or just let them heal over time.

Everything that bothers us, has a solution in us, in our surroundings. The load gets lighter when we carry it well. Pressing too hard and doubting, we can achieve things that cause us frustration; challenges will be greater.

✦ **Quote of the Day:** With patience and a cool head, you can be certain that challenges will be met, even without knowing what solution shall lead you to success. You must know how to set aside whatever is out of your hands, things that due to their nature you cannot change.

DAY 28

What is right today may not be so in the future.

The ability to do the right thing will depend on the perception and understanding of the truth.

Do not look at achieving a goal, as your final effort; rather view it as the first step toward victories to come.

✦ **Quote of the Day:** This world is so complete that even if you stumble, you will always be victorious. It just depends on you, your correction and confidence.

DAY 29

Addictions are not just the ones that eat us away physically and materially; but we must take care regarding the ones that affect us spiritually.

Doubts are human, they will always appear; but spiritual assurance is stronger than emotional doubt. Doubts are a big obstacle to self-esteem and success.

✦ **Quote of the Day:** Be assured of your abilities, as you are the Creator's image.

DAY 30

Life is an art where scenarios are available for performances.

Opportunities are there to be activated; it is up to us to make them a continuing success.

How come? We must go into action in the spiritual realm, to see how the curtain opens on the material plane.

Let's not forget that materiality will not have a place in the intangible world of the spirit. Harmony between material and spiritual is the Compass of success.

⊕ **Quote of the Day:** Spiritual paths leave no room for fear or doubt. Keep walking forward and you will notice the change.

CHAPTER V

MAY
THE REASON TO EXIST IS PERCEPTIBLE

Humanity has always been a tangible and spiritual world.

In the tangible world, these are abundant: vanity, affliction, imperceptible dreams, lies, daily labor, darkness and insatiability. Behind this world created by the senses is also the world of silence and truth, where there is Joy, abundance and divinity as well.

In a world of intangible dreams, there are many empty words without echo, words of vanity.

There is an old proverb which says: "He who grasps at too much will hold little". Could it be: "That too much materiality will keep one's soul away from good deeds"?

In other words: "One handful of peace is better than two hands filled with affliction".

How much more will we strive to exceed the greatness of others, without even understanding that true greatness will never be found in a tangible world?

How much longer are we going to yearn for vanity without realizing our greed?

When you truly understand your "reason to exist"; you will know that the Creator also gave us a gift of joy, even from our efforts, but not from our insatiability.

We shall not forget that joy feeds the spirit and that we never have enough of enjoyment. Joy fills you with contentment and happiness as well; it has a divine nature. Enjoyment comes and goes, brings disharmony and unrest; yet is part of human nature as well.

DAY 1

The only work that is not done in vain, is the abundance of spirit which releases all pain without letting us depart empty.

Material abundance, even when well-guarded has no a guarantee; we came without possessions and so we shall return. The Compass is depart without a bare and empty spirit.

⊕ **Quote of the Day:** Earthly affairs do not give joy to the soul and spirit, but darkness, pain and misery.

DAY 2

Do you remember the day when the Creator filled your life with joy? There is no reason to complain, as He has already shown us that He will always be there.

When we get to the understanding that living is not a chaotic privilege, we will be assured that the solution is in believing. Then the ability to solve and understand everything will be reinforced.

⊕ **Quote of the Day:** Fighting for a physical solution makes no sense, as sooner or later we will depart, the point is to save your soul. If you keep this motto, the Creator will let you be for your own good.

DAY 3

The one who causes discord (anger) and does not know how to stop strife is equally foolish compared to the one whose anger prevents things from get better (by seeing the solution).

They are men unreliable due to their pride, arrogance, foolishness and merciless actions toward others.

✠ **Quote of the Day:** Collective fulfillment becomes a selfish pleasure when it benefits solely one individual.

DAY 4

Often we have been advised: "When you do not know what to do, do not do it". Shall we keep our arms crossed then? No, we simply have to be in harmony before moving towards the unknown.

Opportunities and success are there to obtain. We not need try to comprehend; we only have to aim on reaching them, with patience and humility.

✠ **Quote of the Day:** When the loop is tight, it is because you have pulled it.

DAY 5

Wishes are only achieved with self-confidence. Scrutiny and too much knowledge will not secure a win, much less an emotional release (happiness) if you do not walk with humility.

The Compass is in having firm steps towards our spiritual evolution, like confidence and faith in the Creator.

Following the steps of ego, is seeking glory and self-pleasure, and is judging without knowledge of the truth.

⊕ **Quote of the Day:** Trust is nothing more than accepting yours harmonious nature and living in divine truth, "The light".

DAY 6

When we live for ourselves, we are based on the ego; even when we keep our hopes, dreams and desires under control, we have no truth. The ego is not compatible with prayers; they will not be answered since one cannot pray just according to our own will; but only with certainty and humility.

⊕ **Quote of the Day:** Never choose for yourself alone, if this choice is not a harmonious deed. Do not seek to do only your will.

DAY 7

Joy harmonizes the soul, leaves doubt behind and encourages us. It is like a heavenly energy that makes us resistant to all negativity.

Sadness involves the prospect of a future in darkness and deprives the soul of its aspirations; is like living chained to negativity and mental paralysis as well.

Heavenly energy gives wings while melancholy gives heavy wheels.

⊕ **Quote of the Day:** Full realization is reached; when you realize that your first goal as a divine being is to be "Happy".

DAY 8

Human character is not formed without experiences, good or bad.

We rebel against things that are like instruments that help us shape our character and the ones that fulfill us, should make us humble. The combination of these two, will perfect us with a spiritual power.

⊕ **Quote of the Day:** Imperfection is the basis for your human magnificence, perfection is not born, and it is made.

DAY 9

Great personages have forged their spiritual path with sacrifice and humility, with the ability to love and forgive.

Grandparents used to say, "Be careful with the spine that comes out of the same branch because it will hurt you the most"; perhaps: "If there is no thorn that hurts you, be concerned, since there is no transformation without obstacles."

⊕ **Quote of the Day:** If you prune, you will be leafier.

DAY 10

Emotions will release you and thoughts will bind you.

There is nothing wrong when thoughts lead us to the past or project us into the future; what is wrong is when they alienate us from the present.

Thinking and acting with consciousness and feelings is not the same as doing it with the senses.

⊕ **Quote of the Day:** Keep your eyes on the road. Be vigilant with your own thoughts and wary to embrace foreign thoughts; this will prevent you from going back to the road already traveled.

DAY 11

What makes you think there is nothing negative in us, if everything that exists has its own opposite?

As we acknowledge the negative in our surroundings and the wrongs between us, we will be able to confront and recognize them, and adopt a way to eliminate them; it is the path to positive harmony within a spiritual growth.

✦ **Quote of the Day:** Your negative aspects are there so you can be transformed, not for you judge yourself.

DAY 12

Perseverance makes the difference between a frustrated winner and a successful one.

A frustrated winner, is like a faded rainbow that appeared once and no longer shines. A successful person is like the star that shines by its own light, unique and whose shine will last thorough time.

✦ **Quote of the Day:** The frustrated one is animated by his ego, while the successful one is motivated by the wisdom of being complete.

DAY 13

You can age without growth, as a result of our being isolated internally and externally, when we do not learn thorough time, when we cannot foresee our future, and when by gone tears have erased any present joy.

✦ **Quote of the Day:** Do not remain inert too long; it may shorten your life.

DAY 14

Personal dissatisfaction is on the same path of misunderstanding about existence.

Errors, (anything that causes us harm) create a constant barrier of existential dissatisfaction, leading us toward ephemeral material pleasures; any inner happiness and satisfaction will fill us.

✦ **Quote of the Day:** Inner emptiness is not filled without change. There is only one answer: "Stop searching outside, find yourself".

DAY 15

Errors become problems when we do not realize we can correct them.

The Compass in life, is to affirm that everything will be for better and good.

The only challenge we will face without being victorious is death.

Challenges bring a constant transformation, which have the primary objective of fortifying us spiritually; to be prepared for our reality: "The good death".

✦ **Quote of the Day:** Ask yourself and imagine how boring your life would probably be, without the constant challenge of getting to know life. Challenges are the perfect balance to our lives.

DAY 16

Spirituality, is far from being a physical law, in that it has no attraction of opposite's poles. In its positivity, (good vibes) it only attracts the positive. When we are on spirituality's path, no negative influence will affect us; as we find out that the physical part of our being is the source of our limitation, we find our perfection and our ability to positivism.

✠ **Quote of the Day:** The physical part weakens you and the spiritual part strengthens you.

DAY 17

Human thinking becomes large when we move it away from all limitation; this is achieved only when we think as spiritual beings.

There is no irrationality, anger, contempt, frustration, or hateful thought if we have a good perception of life. There are no errors, we do not get offended, and we live in continual peace, which reflects in our surroundings, and there is a philanthropic feeling toward others.

✠ **Quote of the Day:** Daily routine may eat you away. Do not forget your spiritual essence.

DAY 18

Do not turn our ways of blessing into sophist labyrinths.

The daily walk may or may not bring big challenges, but in essence, is part of the route already established for good, our design.

The extra effort will bring more satisfaction than the laziness of "Don't do it".

✠ **Quote of the Day:** Strive spiritually and do not be discouraged by the ups and downs that take you away from the "Good living".

DAY 19

The physical laws of rotation, translation, and transformation are also part of our human nature.

We are not inert beings. We are not entire beings. The process of physical transformation begins before gestation; but the spiritual is activated for our self, with consciousness.

We are the result of creative energy, and as such, we are in constant evolution. When we follow the flow, we are removing the limits from our great energy, which creates and transforms everything. It doesn't destroy.

⊕ **Quote of the Day:** Stay in constant motion, (mental, physical and spiritual) only then you will see your true transformation in becoming a vessel of light.

DAY 20

The expression, "This is better than nothing," is the basis of failure and a limitation against reaching a destiny of absolute realization. Where there is a balance between giving and receiving, there is no room for collective conformism.

Sharing sets the collective foundation, helps to project us beyond the self; doing the best and receiving the best from our surroundings.

⊕ **Quote of the Day:** Unconditional sharing will open the door of blessings.

DAY 21

The degree of understanding a religion doesn't make a spiritual being.

Being a spiritual being is achieved according to the measure of mercy to understand, accept, and to forgive others as well.

Spirituality is a collective individuality. One cannot be looking for a spiritual evolution if we ignore the needs of others and refuse to share without prejudice; one must step away from the egocentric mind set.

✠ **Quote of the Day:** Constant spiritual work will cast away shadows and limitations. Ups and downs strengthen your fullness; they are not a test to prove your perfection.

DAY 22

Peace and happiness are generated within.

A life full of accomplishments brings balance to our existence, creating the basis for happiness.

The Compass is to remember that happiness is centered on a "Re": Responsibility and Realization; but not in a vacuous fullness, similar to a parched land thirsty for water.

✠ **Quote of the Day:** The neighbor's wall may be lower than your obsession, when your needs and accomplishments are not satisfied.

DAY 23

A thunderstorm may appear light when compared to a long summer day.

How big but beneficial was your fall yesterday, since you are still alive?

Do not hide, as the trace of the boat in the middle of a lake, due to a frustration or an ephemeral fall. The worst type of slavery is the one, where the mind is dominated by fear and ego.

The Compass is on not fleeing from challenges, no matter how big they may be.

✦ **Quote of the Day:** Those are there for a reason. You overcome them and collect a reward. Reach out!

DAY 24

The essence of thinking is the freedom over itself.

How come? When its power is controlled; its greatness is absolute freedom of action; with no room for doubt, negativity and limitation.

A doubtful thought is like a soul's termite; which destroys everything and turns it to dust before good can reach us. Certainty creates and transforms everything.

✦ **Quote of the Day:** There are no physical or spiritual limitations. Life is to be and to succeed in everything.

DAY 25

Yesterday was another bad day?

Let's begin by analyzing how often our words were offensive instead of comforting ones.

Words, like actions, have an echo; but on the cosmic level; for that reason destiny is the result of our past actions.

Change begins in ourselves; setting the basis for a harmonious environment, giving us a daily feeling of been pleased.

✥ **Quote of the Day:** Look always for your essence and keep it healthy.

DAY 26

Lying sentence us doubly: First, we harm ourselves and secondly, because we harm others. Everything will be encased in darkness.

Lying, creates our own jail, limitation and anxiety, as we created them we believe in them, and we are far away from accepting ourselves. As the ego gets bigger, truth diminishes.

✥ **Quote of the Day:** Honesty begins in you.

DAY 27

A problem becomes that, when we do not accept its reality, forgetting that the solution will emerge after we recognize that it exist.

The process of changing that overwhelming is not difficult, at the change begins with small steps first; like carbon becoming diamond.

Once the dark side (problems or what harm us) is accepted, we must initiate a process with patience thorough time; this will make us shine (strengthening).

✥ **Quote of the Day:** Trees are not born lush, already bearing fruit. Begin to plant your crops.

DAY 28

We should not mix stubbornness with resistance.

Resistance makes us great with constant success; stubbornness limits us with constant mistakes. When we perceive beyond human nature, weakness turns into strength, the impossible into possible and dreams becomes true.

The balance between our physical effort and our spiritual freedom is the foundation for a life of miracles.

⊕ **Quote of the Day:** The Compass relies on resisting wisely. Be able to accept and appreciate that which is the essence of good living.

DAY 29

The reflection of our silhouette in the mirror shouldn't be so much our concern, it is only a vision; the reflection of our actions in the cosmos is the flashing or obscuring on the daily life.

The answers about existence are inner, answers about life are in everything around us. Knowing how to combine them, for good, is what makes us a better person.

⊕ **Quote of the Day:** If you dislike your reality, you must consciously change the way you act; you will then see how reality changes its meaning and direction as well. You must try it and let your cosmic reflection shine!

DAY 30

The process of self-discovery, focuses on two aspects: Recognize the positive side (talents, gifts and prosperity) with humility and acceptance, our negative side with determination to change. The combination of the two aspects will set the basis for success.

⊕ **Quote of the Day:** What bothers you now will not necessarily become failure.

DAY 31

We were not born to self-destruct, but to become complete as spiritual beings.

This pattern is intrinsic to human nature; but not in the spiritual realm. To be self-destructive comes from a state of unconsciousness; this, as a consequence, pulls us away from a harmonious spiritual life. Soul it is not. The entity becomes a material body without constructive emotions. When the soul comes into action, we turn away from our instincts.

⊕ **Quote of the Day:** Truth is within you; as you build your destiny, you will understand your design.

CHAPTER VI

JUNE
INVALUABLE WORTH

The eternal soul is of more worth, such as the perception of mortality.

It is a common evil to be like fire which is never satiated; man is blessed with riches and honor, but he still falls into the fallacy of vanity.

There is a state of enjoyment that conceals the divine existence of such emptiness and unrest; where a grave waits for the soul, in its expected departure, and even the name will be forgotten.

An ephemeral world, where the soul didn't find its light, its truth.

What destiny awaits the one who concealed his folly with many words and the one who patiently waited and his mouth never pronounced a word to satisfy himself?

The one who finds the truth, his light, will find rest; the one who was wise, (rich or poor) who knew how to walk, without letting his mouth be filled with desires.

Desire brings bondage, is human, mortal, afflicts the soul, makes us imperfect and carries us to a world of perceivable vanity.

Longing delivers us, is spiritual, immortal, strengthens the soul, brings to us closer to our divine creation, and open doors to a world of imperceptible energy, evolutionary transformation.

What destiny awaits the man who doesn't understand and wants to contend with what is more powerful force than him?

All is said and done each new day; everything is already named.

DAY 1

Everything that is obtained easily, pleases and causes much joy, makes us feel important, winners and cunning; more so than the ones that have not achieved yet. We may pause for a moment and ask the question, how bountiful we are, and how valuable was the effort?

⊕ **Quote of the Day:** Everything that satisfies you momentarily is transitory and worthless, so will your happiness be.

DAY 2

Sharing will not make us subservient beings, but rather when we do it, without obligation, we have learned and activated the essence of giving and receiving.

We should not confuse servility with serving. The first one involves humiliation and the second magnifies the self in its evolution. Servility is limitation, while serving delivers us, and there is no ego.

✥ **Quote of the Day:** That which you are looking for, be recognized it, and when you release it magnifies you, is the "Ego".

DAY 3

Blaming others for our lack of accomplishment is not the way.

The law of cause and effect works also in us. We will never obtain our yearnings if we are not prepared to receive; and even if we get there, it will only be temporary.

✥ **Quote of the Day:** Self-realization is within you; not based on the comfort others may can give you.

DAY 4

You can have it all and lack appreciation; or you can also be filled with gratitude for only a few possessions. Wealth is not the source of happiness, much less a fruit tree of blessings.

✥ **Quote of the Day:** You can have the best coffin; but it will not be filled with your richness.

DAY 5

Searching involves movement; nothing will be found if you stay in the same place.

A difficult profession for a man is constant learning in the path of change.

Learning to know ourselves may cause pain; physical pain doesn't make us slaves, but being afraid to change does. We should not stop accepting challenges that seem insuperable; the fact that we recognize them makes us stronger, it builds confidence and self-esteem.

✠ **Quote of the Day:** Slavery is feeding on conformism.

DAY 6

We have spent a lifetime looking for something that we cannot find.

Would our own denials and fear to correct errors propel us to a new beginning? That denial perhaps don't let us see the simplicity of truth. The search and answer are within us.

✠ **Quote of the Day:** The important thing is not to find the answer; but knowing what to do with it.

DAY 7

Shouting and noises are heard; whispers and the melodies are listened for. One may hear with the ears, but must listen with the soul. When we hear there is no reasoning; when we listen there is understanding. Hearing is instinctive, listening is human. Hearing distracts you and listening instructs you; hearing may embarrass us, while the art of listening elevates us.

Hearing of others needs does not result in humility if it doesn't get to our conscience; it is there when we are vulnerable to the pain of others.

✠ **Quote of the Day:** If sharing has not made you a better person, it is because you are not trying your best.

DAY 8

Words can create stories, while others are irrational, that obstruct change, and thus the evolution of being.

✦ **Quote of the Day:** Pay attention to the spoken word; the answer to your concern may come from the least expected voice. A word that is ignored perhaps limits your existence.

DAY 9

Make no mistake, having our needs met doesn't mean that we are getting what we want.

A gap in our needs is the result of our own fears and the loss of confidence in ourselves.

Fear is lack, love is abundance; fear makes us judge, and by doing this we put limitations on our needs (as beings of light) to evolve with them.

When we love ourselves, our potential and confidence having grown, we walk through a path of plentitude and satisfaction.

Needs are fulfilled and yearnings are satisfied in our spiritual life.

✦ **Quote of the Day:** Perseverance overcomes circumstances; is the gift of your courage.

DAY 10

Where there is justice; there may not necessarily be kindness.

Justice is reflexive, represses and places limits on the senses. Kindness is a whole feeling, comprehensive, and gives freedom to the senses.

Acting with justice doesn't mean that we have goodness in our hearts; judgmental sight will limit the existence of being; gradually closes doors of blessings around us.

✥ **Quote of the Day:** How do you want to be regarded with kindness and equality, if you do not sowed mercy in your being?

DAY 11

How do we know we walk in the correct path of transformation?

When today's actions are far from yesterday's actions. To be more accurate, we say to ourselves: this will not happen again, I want to correct this mistake, and how could this have happened?

As we recall, there is only one way for the correction and the option is intrinsic to our only destiny. The correction is our decision; one more lesson in life.

✥ **Quote of the Day:** The right actions are the ones that cause no harm.

DAY 12

Things happen to us as they are and have been destined.

They are the result of something that was created before; be it by our actions or the actions of others.

The way that we receive, experience and accept them, depends on our level of consciousness; as well as, the level of damage or good that we receive.

Everything is a development for the encounter with our own consciousness, our existence.

✢ **Quote of the Day:** There will be no negative outcome coming your way, when you walk the path of harmony, truth and spirituality.

DAY 13

What bothers us now will not necessarily become defeat tomorrow.

We must then learn how to swim over adversity to avoid sinking into the sea of spirituality.

The Compass is to gain strength during adversity, (constraints) which are certain to happen even if we are spiritual and in harmony with our surroundings. We must not deny the fact but seek its cause and learn the lesson it carries.

✢ **Quote of the Day:** Accept bad happenings at the proper time, your second reminder will be much bigger. Change awaits you for your good; you must accept it.

DAY 14

Art is the human form in which the light of the Creator is expressed.

Art begins to do damage when our ego is manifested.

The weakness of the self will show when we are not giving our best and certainly the beauty's art will be lost.

✢ **Quote of the Day:** Even when you think you are the best artist in the world; that will not guarantee you spiritual growth, while you think you are the creator of your art; you are actually just the channel of the divine expression.

DAY 15

Humiliation sets the base for humility and greatness of spirit.

When we walk the path of peace, light and wisdom, other people's offenses will make us stronger.

Woe to those who use their own power to humiliate and impoverish the spirit of others; leaving their own spirits thirsty and behind. They carry so much confusion and don't understand that their angry words will magnify their own agony.

⊕ **Quote of the Day:** Do not despise the servant who begins to reign in his own true.

DAY 16

Do not seek to understand moments of unrest; just accept them as part of your own evolution.

The search for the essence of perfection from them for us, is the Compass.

The first step in coping with the pain, bewilderment and confusion is to let them finish their course. "After the storm comes the calm", says the phrase. While we look to be better at what we already are; we must get rid of the obstacles in the way and become harmonious beings of light.

⊕ **Quote of the Day:** Opportunities come in different shades; but the simplest will surely be the most risky.

DAY 17

The power of thought stops being a mystery when it is mastered; bringing as a result, the revival of the spirit.

When we stay still, silence sharpens our perception and intuition takes over, in a free harmonious will.

⊕ **Quote of the Day:** Never hesitate, and you will make a good decision.

DAY 18

There is no problem without a solution, as there is not an unanswered question; all is a matter of attitude. When our conscience is focus, the solution real and the answer is clear; it was always there, in the light.

The Compass is in understanding that the only meaningful things worthy to accumulate for our lives, are the experiences not the frustrations.

⊕ **Quote of the Day:** Each obstacle we overcome, is the manifestation of a miracle.

DAY 19

We shall not be satisfied with what has been achieved; we should also aim for what it hasn't become yet, giving more of ourselves. It is something like letting go with the flow of pristine water; in constant movement and purification, without blockage.

The thoughts, actions and experiences that focus on our self, have one single purpose, to make our existence productive, as well as collective.

⊕ **Quote of the Day:** The accumulation of experiences shared on the road, gives us knowledge and the meaning of what is valuable in life; as ignorance and errors are eliminated this way.

DAY 20

The lack of understanding existence, the meaning of the life and the challenge to have a harmonious earthly interaction; can lead to sadness.

When frustrations build up from an early age and after, they manifest in panic attacks.

What do we do then? We ought not look, but observe; not hear, but listen. We should not feel but perceive; not despise, but love. Ours is not to possess, but to share and always have open arms to help; likewise to receive and accept from the ones who day to day are ahead of us.

⊕ **Quote of the Day:** Let your soul wake up every morning, it will guide you to a secure port.

DAY 21

What comes easily doesn't build us up; rather it makes us vulnerable and in the same easy way it leaves. When we have persistence in something, we are building a foundation and we gain knowledge that will be hardly stripped.

All is part of transcending over an unconditional will. Those happenings shape us as beings; without ruling out that our conscious ability to interact with the environment has influence also.

⊕ **Quote of the Day:** You are the cause and you have the power to control your search to be transformed; there are no worthless facts, moments, or circumstantial people in your surroundings.

DAY 22

It may sound contradictory but the degree of understanding and knowledge we have, will dictate the value we give to our environment and our possessions; whether of if they were acquired by our own effort or the effort of others. In other words, the revelation is there, we see it, we understand it, but there is no meaning if we do not capture its essence.

To act and to think with consciousness is not the same as doing it with the senses.

⊕ **Quote of the Day:** Consciousness is the rational soul, the one that releases you and carries the truth. The human senses are irrational; they limit you and take you to the reality of your ego and sophistry.

DAY 23

The first step to eliminate the ego is to accept what embarrasses us; by accepting our faults we will understand their existence and their purpose.

When we understand their goal, we resolve them, as we resolve them we magnify, and by doing this we grow as well.

Growing in harmony will not limit us, as we are free in mind and spirit. Then there is no ego, as a limitation, equal to negativity.

⊕ **Quote of the Day:** When there is no ego, others will perceive you more beautifully; your beauty will shine and you will spread brightness with your own light.

DAY 24

Our actions are like the shadow, they follow us at the same step; even if we are in the dark believing nobody can see us.

Actions have a rolling effect, before the cry that nobody thinks about you and nobody understands you; think if you have sown a seed for it.

⊕ **Quote of the Day:** You are not just a grain of sand in the whole, you are as well the cause that creates and destroys with just a "click".

DAY 25

When routine starts wearing us down and we feel like we are drowning in our daily tasks; it is because we are acting according to our "ego".

We must change the tactic and move toward the unconditional "we"; we will notice that each dawn brings a new learning experience.

⊕ **Quote of the Day:** The ego is not a good companion and advisor; when decisions are based on it, you will not achieve a harmonious elevation of your being.

DAY 26

The surrounding reality is not the key factor on our decisions, the one that creates personality.

We can change whatever is harsh for us, and convert a dessert of stones into a fountain of life. The decision is ours to make, and consists in how we apply our thoughts and actions of daily life.

⊕ **Quote of the Day:** Imperfection is part of perfecting the human being at the very moment of accepting it, as a whole, integrated for your benefit.

DAY 27

Many things are lost for lack of patience, and likewise due to waiting too long.

Understanding is achieved by walking through sloth and falsehood; otherwise a dream (sophistry) will cover you.

Laziness is the mother of folly and poverty. Diligence and wealth go hand-in-hand.

⊕ **Quote of the Day:** The Compass is to know where your benefits is, when the world is at your feet. By surrendering to superfluous vanities, more is lost; only understanding and mercy benefit your existence.

DAY 28

Wailing for yesterday's losses closes the door to today's wealth. Avoid that occurrence in your life by increasing your desire for more, but giving more than you receive.

By simply returning a pure feeling of gratitude, rather than assigning a material category to things, you will see how everything in life flows.

⊕ **Quote of the Day:** Where there is harmony, there won't be much need. As all responds to measure, loss will have a replacement.

DAY 29

Living on a fixed program routine can be as deadly as a small box of cigars: they draw us, they urge us, they grab us and quietly we start gasping for air.

We must find the routine that will make us better in every breath, not one that will destroy us, with each one.

Taking spiritual responsibility is the Compass that harmonizes our evolving self.

✥ **Quote of the Day:** Dependency or helping, you decide.

DAY 30

Time goes beyond the human, except for the soul. The soul is eternal, until the physical perception of the self will be manifested with its path of light.

We have the ability to produce good or evil. To do good deeds, is all up to us. There are no conditions, and the Compass is in the good speaking and acting. To do evil, nothing is needs to be provided; we act from our own free will without caring about how harmful to others it can be.

✥ **Quote of the Day:** Spirituality is interior, but shall be reflected outward.

CHAPTER VII

JULY
FOLLY: LIMITATION OF THE EXISTENCE

"Folly does wonders in the mind of the deluded".

In a rational state with understanding about the essence of the self, there is no room for folly. The common man carries his own spirit to an unconscious inertia.

The life of a fool is full of empty words and a haughty ego that feeds on handouts; with principles based on malice, anger, wandering and errors, there is a lack of a harmonious spirit, but not of a suffering one.

The basis of the life without comfort, is not the lack of something; instead is the lack of appreciation for what we already have and our senselessness.

We fall into the fallacy of a life full of riches, and with them we try to create a shield to protect us from the real intrinsic adversity.

A truth enduring through times is that wisdom provides irreplaceable life to the ones who possess it.

Wisdom has its essence in each human being and it is ready to respond to our call at any time we want; as soon as we understand that all is fruitful on the path to light and understanding.

We must not make our lives a routine. Routine and a way of living; they are like water and oil, mixing them is useless, and to separate them is the challenge to success.

DAY 1

Making others believe in us will be possible at the moment we trust in our ability to be. Releasing our fears will impel actions and positive thoughts; opening a world of possibilities.

We must let circumstances flow, and prevent the ones which are like nebulas; those that do not allow us to see the favorable alternatives we must experience and make them our own.

We must understand that our destiny is a rewarding life, with ups and downs that they must make us better humans. The purpose of falls and errors is to expand our good will, in order to reach our spiritual, physical and material plentitude.

⊕ **Quote of the Day:** A being burdened by the absence of the Creator is like an eternal prison. With Him, time and success are yours.

DAY 2

The difference between long term success and trivial success goes beyond the degree of dedication.

As we are able to recognize we are the channel for a demonstration of art and any other talent; we will bring increase to others, not to our irrational ego.

A successful wise person will never have a selfish spirituality.

✦ **Quote of the Day:** We must keep a daily check on our ego before leaving the house. Being sensible will mend soul wounds.

DAY 3

The fake art of the insensate is: To pretend to be wise while in nescience; to hide the true, to lie till the end, to presume to know what cannot be understood, to be what it is not, to ignore what is being spoken, to subsist with ignorance and feign knowing. The insensate searches just for convenience.

✦ **Quote of the Day:** One must have courage even to sink without making noise, and to be able to keep afloat.

DAY 4

Lack of wisdom is the foundation of insensate insolence and arrogance. We must not trust their assumption as a righteous path and success; because like a volatile temperament, success will be short, and happiness therefore will be cut.

✦ **Quote of the Day:** Where there is foolishness, there is not understanding and much less reason.

DAY 5

Envy is manifested by the lack of appreciation of what surrounds us, whether we own it or not; we are not satiated. We feel miserable beyond the material, in the spirit.

Envy is a negative feeling which only has its remedy within us.

When we rely on others for a solution to our problems, the way becomes frustrating.

⊕ **Quote of the Day:** There is no room for materiality in the intangible spiritual world.

DAY 6

Have you ever seen wisdom in foolishness?

The fool is so clumsy that he even flaunts his folly using the only ability he has to dishonor his neighbor. Only with wisdom you will prevail, with it we have the ability to create for good, and the creation is affirmed with intelligence.

⊕ **Quote of the Day:** Do not seek to do what is already done; learn to enrich with what lays ahead of you.

DAY 7

Humility helps you accept; and the ego makes you deny. Loving is accepting; judging is rejecting. When we reject we go far from our spiritual nature and we cling to our human side.

⊕ **Quote of the Day:** When you do not know the essence of your life, you will dissipate hopelessly to a world of senseless vanity; you will pass to an anonymous existential state.

DAY 8

The most precious miracle of creation is us and is within us.

We are seeds of the tree of life, which is full of miraculous fruits; according to the roots.

We must cultivate generosity, loyalty, compassion and love, no matter how stony the field (life) is.

⊕ **Quote of the Day:** An overwhelmed spirit will manifest in your physical nature.

DAY 9

Are there any mistakes, defects or baseness too difficult to be overcome? No! A human being has the ability to be receptive to any knowledge, which helps him to connect and ascend with the truth (destiny), in his pure liberty; without folly and unreason.

Every human being is suitable for understanding and wisdom.

✠ **Quote of the Day:** Ignorance as well as rebellion will lead to a path of destruction and spiritual death; the Compass is on keeping the "ego" under control.

DAY 10

Inexpressible gaiety is the eternal joy; a repetitive transient playfulness is the common, earthly one. The inexpressible gaiety is obtained by letting the eternal human essence manifest itself, through our physical being. When understanding opens the door to true knowledge, we are freed from spiritual captivity; our divine nature emerges.

✠ **Quote of the Day:** There is no physical or material limitation, neither professional nor social, that limits your divine joy; it is innate and it manifestation depends on you.

DAY 11

We shall not confuse the term 'being more' with 'having more'.

Being more is a constant receiving; having more is just a material state.

Discovering and accepting our spiritual needs and faults will not guarantee us a harmonious evolution; we must do it with conscience.

✦ **Quote of the Day:** Remember to get rid of faults with the aim to convert them into a quality during your spiritual growth.

DAY 12

When we are dealing with confusing thoughts, we console ourselves by saying "Better times will come".

The truth is, that if we do not work towards our plentitude now, we will not have a present and better time. There is no after for happiness, but always a now.

✦ **Quote of the Day:** It will only depend of you and your actions, not on others or in pleasant circumstances.

DAY 13

Egocentrism is a synonym of lack, selfishness and senseless. We must know that the verb satisfy implies a humble and contagious prosperity, when it is conjugated with "us". It will thus provide light that brings harmony and abundance.

✦ **Quote of the Day:** The desire to receive for oneself will limit the soul's growth.

DAY 14

An impious prosperity will perturb the soul, but the merciful sharer will nourish it.

The difference between an impious and a righteous man, on the path, is that the wicked transforms his path to perdition and the just charges it to grow more.

A way without sanity is like a land without sense or law; none are guilty; there are simply losers with no forgiveness. There, hatred and senselessness sustain grudges forever.

✠ **Quote of the Day:** The impious will never sacrifice himself; but the just will be willing, and his spirit will thrive with joy.

DAY 15

How many times have we said, that there is no peace in our lives? Have we been merciful with our surroundings; seeking the personal or collective truth?

We dishonor ourselves with senseless stepping into anguish, which leads us to an internal conflict that affects our surroundings. The Compass is on finding the true knowledge.

✠ **Quote of the Day:** Your conduct is the reflection of your knowledge; according to the path taken with or without reason. Your reason goes hand in hand with your understanding.

DAY 16

Righteousness and wisdom paths; are based on "prudence".

Folly is not the basis of wisdom, but rather of intolerance and ignorance. The foolish one acts and speaks without prudence and lacks respect for himself and others.

✠ **Quote of the Day:** The fall of the foolish is unavoidable, and is easy to identify; the more riches they have, the more wrecked their lives are.

DAY 17

When one looks for the negative in the self, one must look as well for a solution.

To find them and let them stay may bring confusion, despair and panic.

The Compass is acts in ceaseless action. Once they are overcome, there is attainment and personal satisfaction, leading to happiness.

⊕ **Quote of the Day:** Overcoming the cause of your misery (negativity and obstacles) is more gratifying and valuable for your spirit than to keep walking in a daily routine.

DAY 18

The person who gets more but without using his own effort, always will be frustrated.

Learning to be a leader of self is the basis for earthly triumph and spiritual success.

There is a difference between triumph and success: Triumph makes us more conscious of our human ability, while success is our true light and reason to exist.

⊕ **Quote of the Day:** Using ballet shoes will not guarantee you'll be a successful dancer.

DAY 19

Strife, discord and wickedness are part of daily life; knowing how to avoid them is part of good living; this is the difference between the righteous and the impious.

The just honor themselves and leave to avoid strife; the wicked act without integrity and remain, being on their own senseless.

⊕ **Quote of the Day:** There is no peace in an insensate heart. Anger and violence will bring grief and sorrow.

DAY 20

Ironic, when we are not criticized negatively, is like don't be we important and not envied by others; even so, it is not a good way to lives. When we accept negative criticism, we rebuild from the inside out.

✛ **Quote of the Day:** Remember that critics are channels used for your good, as long as you are willing to accept you are here to evolve; otherwise you will always have conflicts with your surroundings.

DAY 21

When egocentrism and isolation prevail, self-destructive patterns irradiate within. Our physical nature is already a limitation; that may or not have a lasting joy. The force of the spirit strengthens the soul, not the material possessions.

✛ **Quote of the Day:** Personal dissatisfaction leads to superfluous pleasures; it makes you vulnerable to overcome challenges in your life.

DAY 22

Dissatisfaction and sadness both go in the direction of incomprehensible existence.

Fleeting pleasures surely fill the being with pain; since the understanding is not focused on eliminating errors from the root.

The Compass is start to push away oppressive thoughts, aiming to replace them with our divine destiny, "being happy".

✛ **Quote of the Day:** Unfortunate memories will give you eternal bitterness, if you do not obliterate them.

DAY 23

Fears and temptations that we do not accept and bring under control, will become our own perdition; alternatively to that, they will reveal our truth. When we do not value our worth and success, we are far from happy.

⊕ **Quote of the Day:** Fear is distrust, confusion and an easy path to addiction; happiness is your right, accept it.

DAY 24

Life is like a puzzle, which gives you satisfaction just to see the landscape that emerges when you finally assert yourself, after errors, and put the pieces together.

⊕ **Quote of the Day:** Move beyond as in a simple table game. Persevere!

DAY 25

Happenings are overwhelming and sometimes hard to express, especially when prayers cannot be express, when feelings are really confusing and greater.

Not deviating from good counsel, is like a shelter and light on your path; even when it seems confusing, they will prevail.

⊕ **Quote of the Day:** You must listen to avoid making mistakes; here is the Compass, getting away from the foolishness that don't allow you to express yourself. Swift and idle people, nothing discovering; time turns vile against them, as they grow more and more torpid.

DAY 26

Envy is a synonym of self-destruction, rooted in our fear; it is also the antonym of happiness.

✦ **Quote of the Day:** True relationships are part of our challenge for the sake of good achievements in harmony.

DAY 27

We would be fulfilled if we succeeded in changing one by one the negative aspects of our personality.

To take a first step to success, time is not the obstacle, but fearful indecision is.

✦ **Quote of the Day:** Remember to start from the smallest of your negative cargo.

DAY 28

Success is a constant challenge, with no room to look back.

It could be limited too, if, once obtained, we fear the future; so we ask ourselves: What comes next?

✦ **Quote of the Day:** There are dreams which are not worthy of realizing, those unharmonious ones; they will become nightmares from which you awaken in failure, at the end of the wrong road.

DAY 29

Energy that comes from giving and sharing is so strong and transcendental, such as comes from forgiving; dissolves any internal and surrounding negativity.

Art of giving shall be harmonious, act of kindness. How do we notice it is a harmonious act? It is when joy and plentitude emerge at the moment of doing it; without nuisance, anguish or discomposure.

✥ **Quote of the Day:** Giving has no title, friendship or relationship; is simply natural, like walking.

DAY 30

Changing the daily routine of our acts and transcending the logical, is eliminating chaos.

Change opens a door to new possibilities and the plentitude ability will multiplied.

Routine is intrinsic to the egocentric human nature; that overshadows the real need of the soul. We must be alert to perceive the intrinsic search calling. How does that happen?

✥ **Quote of the Day:** Do not free the certainty that there is something more there. Step without fear, everything is manifesting before your eyes ... The time is now!

DAY 31

We become greater when we feel the need to accept with thanks everything that happens to us.

Daily life is a constant challenge to our skills; where there is no multiple choice or any answer applies. The right answer (right path) is unique: Learn the lesson and move on.

✥ **Quote of the Day:** Take the fact, analyze it and accept it, thus you will be purified and enriched with harmonious experiences.

CHAPTER VIII

AUGUST
WISDOM OR NOTHING

To embark on a life path without expecting wisdom is like depriving oneself of sleep. Suffering from confusion will affect us for a lifetime.

When we do not apply wisdom in our lives, we become incapable of kindness, and wickedness will be our slavery; the spirit lacks harmony.

Accepting the shadow of iniquity is the same as doing evil by intention; days of fallacy will follow.

The wicked one acts without any sense of right or wrong; even if someone lends him knowledge, he will never flourish.

Iniquity is the only state in life where the lack of fear leads to perdition; in it, there is no bliss and no peace other than being oblivious to wisdom.

Wisdom brightens the face and we perceive clarity with it, we discern time and judgment for the things that we want.

When we have knowledge of good acts and deeds, we have as well understanding about the works that only the Creator may achieve.

Constant and collective wisdom work gets projected with the harmony and elevation of all existing beings in the world. We are a spiritual collective whole, yet still individuals.

Wisdom strengthens the spirit during adversity.

DAY 1

Wisdom creates a better world when shared; otherwise it becomes selfishness, and ironically, will lead to a sea of errors, and a life full of prejudices or biases.

Whatever is wise, needs to be captured in the soul, this is needed in order to have a life full of conscience, with a purpose of humility and shared spirituality.

⊕ **Quote of the Day:** Undisclosed wisdom will not make you a better person; nor will it make wisdom flourish.

DAY 2

Comfort is the opposite of stress, due to personal transformation. When we feel the urge to strive, we add more value to our actions.

Having everything doesn't guarantee the joy of the soul. Excessive comfort is an obstacle to wisdom. A responsible knowledge to act right, and for good, is what leads to a path of plentitude.

⊕ **Quote of the Day:** Human decay occurs as soon as men forget love and misunderstand the whole creation.

DAY 3

There are two kinds of intelligent people; the wise and unwise, they who scoff at the misfortune of others and ignore the truth that understanding must be shared.

How can we expect to find open doors if we as well keep ours shut even though someone is waiting?

✦ **Quote of the Day:** Inferior intelligence seeks, from harming others, to benefit its own convenience.

DAY 4

Discounting value of wisdom is to allow darkness to shelter the "soul".

There is then no room for justice and truth, but for a veil and a life of vain illusions; it happens with separation from the unseen, especially faith and spirituality.

✦ **Quote of the Day:** The body is a type of limited life; it sustains you, but doesn't release you.

DAY 5

Man has the capability of reaching more and more; but his inner greatness will be revealed according to what his soul has achieved, as this will represent him before the Creator.

Having gratitude for the small things is like tuning one's perspective and thus avoiding beforehand whatever is harmful for the soul.

✦ **Quote of the Day:** Everything can be stripped away due to lack of gratitude.

DAY 6

There is a compelling difference between a wise man who is humble and a magnificent one decorated with offal. Humility doesn't make us poor, but pride can fill us with offal. Humility is the base of prudence and truth; with them you are satisfied in abundance. The arrogant are not prudent and are far from the truth.

✤ **Quote of the Day:** Wisdom: Not to exonerate the wicked, nor to convict the righteous.

DAY 7

The wise man knows how to combine obligation, pleasure and necessity; without falling into an excess of any of them.

Modesty is a virtue in the human being; even so, for the insatiable, it is just a disadvantage.

✤ **Quote of the Day:** When avarice frames your happiness, you will be hopelessly lost.

DAY 8

Words have their essence and as such can cause harm as well as good. When they are ejected like a boomerang; they will come back.

Words and thoughts thrive on the bustle of the ego or the whisper of the soul.

✤ **Quote of the Day:** Pay no attention to hear-say, perhaps you'll hear something about yourself, that may not be to your liking.

DAY 9

Before rejecting or heeding to any advice, you must analyze its source or the essence it manifests.

Critiques are not destructive, but camouflaged advice from which we can draw a compliment. Learning how to negate those beneficious, is the Compass.

⊕ **Quote of the Day:** Fret if you do not receive advice; it may be you are not putting forth even minimal effort.

DAY 10

Wisdom may seem confusing to others, when they don't ask for it; it is prudence, as well, which avoids damage.

To some, the basis of a wrong life is the lack of courage to seek the truth; therefore, "do not despise the milk if you dislike butter".

⊕ **Quote of the Day:** The impossible becomes possible when you understand your perfection; it will be possible when you live with confidence and strength, walking the path of wisdom righteousness.

DAY 11

The expression, "Love others as yourself", is not well understood if we do not apply it and put it into practice.

The difference between death and hatred is that hatred ends spiritually and death ends physically; the similarity among them is that grudges' absolute darkness will depart with us.

⊕ **Quote of the Day:** Keep in mind the power of these three: Love, Appreciation, and Self-esteem if you really want to save your spiritual destiny

DAY 12

Do not let your left hand know what your right hand is doing.

Let the need to give flow without expecting anything in return. When we realize that the word "give" is synonymous to flow, we will be spiritual and free from all that is material and spiritual.

✦ **Quote of the Day:** To have or have not may restrict the flow of harmonious abundance.

DAY 13

When we have more than what is needed, we acquiesce in others, penury or poverty. An emerging conformity and custom, will always spell emptiness.

When we do not get what we want, we are expecting a miracle; i.e. we are not acting in the necessary and total search, to complete our plentitude.

✦ **Quote of the Day:** You will always have what you need to complete your spiritual work on your way to plentitude.

DAY 14

Is easier to find a religious person who is spiritual than a spiritual person who is religious.

Religion is a doctrine that can be converted into an ordinary mechanical routine, if we let materiality decide for us. Spirituality however is a constant liberation from this material world; thus our decisive actions will not be limited and much less a step back in a harmonious truth.

✦ **Quote of the Day:** Failing to accept your surroundings will make you more vulnerable.

DAY 15

The soul is like a car; if you do not keep it in good condition, it will never lead you to the desired place. Unlike a car, we do not have to drive it; let it act on autopilot and feel the peace.

✦ **Quote of the Day:** Although the road be full of obstacles, you will arrive in optimal condition.

DAY 16

We must not compare will with liberty. The will is a manifestation of the ego; showing control of the circumstances, when what is really happening is the opposite.

With freedom there is no control of circumstances; simply the ability to understand and resolve them fundamentally, when necessary, without limitations.

✦ **Quote of the Day:** Falling becomes a felt experience when we act freely; there is no confusion and life is bearable and full.

DAY 17

All credibility is not certainty.

We must worry about doubts, concerns and questions, when we don't have them.

We are in a constant process of change and ascension. We must choose a world of harmony and assurance; as this chaotic world has false answers and simple routine ways, which lead us to an intrinsic irrational cycle of mere survival.

✦ **Quote of the Day:** The Compass will affirm that you are qualified to achieve your goals and be a lasting winner.

DAY 18

Peace begins when we allow to ourselves our own evolution, understanding thus how important it is to pass on to others the same right.

In the evolution, there are no barriers to a harmonious character development.

⊕ **Quote of the Day:** You are for all and with all; but unique and independent in your actions and decisions; in your own space.

DAY 19

Our human and universal essence keeps us in a circumstantial circle, which is intrinsic as well.

Everyone has something to offer, and as unique beings, each of us has something different to offer in the harmonious flow of life; once we limit the flow, conflicts arise.

⊕ **Quote of the Day:** Life is a constant yield (sacrifice) and receive, a flow of abundance and projection between the given and the received.

DAY 20

There is a certain irony: That amidst chaos there is order, a reason to be.

The Compass is on knowing how to appreciate as if from outside; so that we can see the true essence of a harmonious order.

That is when we learn to keep our heads, our steps coordinated, and our urges controlled, without thinking of who we are. Why, then, are we hesitant to stop the chaos?

⊕ **Quote of the Day:** If you understand the essence of the truth within you; there is no weakness that you cannot control.

DAY 21

Wisdom is the deep understanding of the universal plan of life; it is the blossoming with the Creator's energy. Wisdom, gives us the spiritual ability to allow that light (universal and creative truth) to manifest itself in our actions with the environment and all living beings.

✦ **Quote of the Day:** Intellectual knowledge is not a precondition to become wise; but to be enlightened, you need to be wise and know yourself.

DAY 22

If we understood that our inner garment has a strong projection, we would spend that extra money in search of a flexible shell in order to be strong against life's difficulties, and sensitive to the pain of others.

The Compass is in understanding that the ego feeds the senses, leaving the emotions without existence.

✦ **Quote of the Day:** The deal is not what I had or will have, but what is in the hand. The right now, shall be our reason to live in harmony with the surroundings.

DAY 23

If you love them, keep still, let them cry, allow them to express and even to act guided by error. Love will be the best advice and even the answer, in these moments of confusion; our words will be less than the imperceptible wind, as they search for their true release.

Just as food has different satisfactions, the same goes for the spirit.

⊕ **Quote of the Day:** You will get the satisfactions to you need, which will make you grow in experience.

DAY 24

Fear limits our initiative to launch our spiritual growth and happiness; affects self-esteem.

Unlike vice, challenges will not make us losers, they are the only addiction that will make us better human beings.

⊕ **Quote of the Day:** You are a being of divine creation. Go forth aware of this and enjoy your harmonious happiness!

DAY 25

Full happiness is the one that doesn't leave a bitter taste in the mouth, nor a void.

Emptiness is a synonym of lack, where darkness dwells; an intangible world of vanities, in no way profound; never satiated, only a resounding negative echo.

⊕ **Quote of the Day:** We all have a second chance to correct past weaknesses.

DAY 26

There is no divine connection, if, knowing the truth, we do not share it.

Virtue is born with good understanding; it creates noble men, those who learn and teach the best. Wisdom is a universal law, by virtue of being available to all; but it is unique and indivisible; an open book, indestructible, easy to grasp and harmonious.

✦ **Quote of the Day:** Wisdom is not a condition for the spiritual part of the self; rather it controls the mind's power.

DAY 27

There are no bad decisions taken; they are simply not experienced yet.

The Compass is to know how understand; living our true destiny, not the other's destiny, and never forget to share. Learning to live and to share is loving; these are the truly human actions which will lead us to a spiritual plentitude.

✦ **Quote of the Day:** Your hands will be filled in accord with what you offered.

DAY 28

Hope moves us forward, but the certainty keep us in the plenteous spiritual life.

Hopes are the result of the short term desires, but the certainty vivified the soul's yearnings; hopes are rooted in logic, while certainty is illogical.

✦ **Quote of the Day:** Do not hesitate, miracles are illogical and irrational as well; because their maker is the divine particle in yourself; in whole.

DAY 29

When we settle for less, we receive less. Only our limited conscious aptitude, unfences our material and spiritual levels.

Blessings always manifest when we need them the most, unless our routine doesn't allow us to appreciate them. They depends in our choices.

❖ **Quote of the Day:** Raise your conscience and wait for more from everything, from you.

DAY 30

Spiritual work begins when you opt for plentitude, receptive and free, without bondage; free of prejudiced thought, actions and words, and living in complete harmony beyond the senses.

❖ **Quote of the Day:** Light carries light, and there is also light in the darkness.

DAY 31

We accept that spirituality exists and can be perceived; but it must be put into practice, otherwise yearnings are merely being collected into an empty sack, leaving no trace. There is no result, and one falls into repetitive beginning minus common sense.

❖ **Quote of the Day:** Blessings will be according to what you keep in your yearnings sack.

CHAPTER IX

SEPTEMBER
TIME THAT HAPPENS

An event occurs alike to everyone, regardless of what is inside the human being.

Our truth, supported within the experience of fullness and joy, builds us as we depart. Our deeds and actions will be our pass to salvation in the face of the Creator.

What happens is in front of our eyes, right and wrong, even when many do not perceive it.

Ordinary man does not recognize the good times; therefore he has no ability to predict the bad time; this will fall on him.

We must understand that this race is not reserved for the swift or the strong, that bread is not solely for the prudent, that wealth is not for the wise only, and that grace is not just for the eloquent; time and occasion happen for everyone.

It is better to be peaceful and wise than brutal and ignorant; thus with wisdom we find release and with silence good words are express. On ignorance, innocuous words are heard and goodness destroyed.

The righteous and his works, the wise and his works, the arrogant and his works, the profane and his works, all of them are part of an earthly creation, having the shadow of a unique and universal whole, the Creator.

It is not what happens to you what creates you, but rather your reactions; reactions feed your divine essence or may destroy you.

Turning the page is done in the here and now; hopes, as well as oblivion, are part of life.

DAY 1

A routine life can limit our evolution as harmonious beings.

It may sound contradictory, but harmony is not a calm routine. By living in harmony we are in a constant movement, positive and energetic, with all that surrounds us.

Giving and receiving, accepting and understanding, loving and living with plentitude we search and we find, we observe and never finish learning. Leaving sense behind is allowing emotion to take over.

⊕ **Quote of the Day:** With the ruler you measure, you will be measured. Do not judge; rather observe, learn and give all you have, even if is not necessary.

DAY 2

We look, perceive as we feel and attract everything that our conscious self wants and seeks within. Everything that happens is a magnet from our energetic center. In that context, the law of attraction applies throughout our existence.

⊕ **Quote of the Day:** Any state of consciousness endures because the universe's energy is dynamic and fluid.

DAY 3

Our living work of art, is born by making things one at the time, with dedication and the assurance that is our best.

Catching birds (challenges) will bring us satisfaction; for the simple expectation that we can go after it and not come back empty handed.

There nothing wrong with yearning for extravagance and material power; the wrong occurs when we abandon our human essence to acquire it.

⊕ **Quote of the Day:** From pleasure we pass to the pain and from ecstasy to agony.

DAY 4

When we search for the reason for our ailment, we are starting a process of self-esteem.

We honor ourselves, when we love and accept ourselves. Acting otherwise, will take us to an inner negation; being dragged toward an abyss of emotional loneliness, pain and panic.

When we know ourselves, we are able to perceive the source of our anguish.

⊕ **Quote of the Day:** Perceive, live and grow, for experiences are process and fears that arise from anxiety are restraints.

DAY 5

We are embraced by history; we can all become heroes. It is not the past, our history; but the reflection of our actions. When we cannot harmonize process of our previous actions, our living present is limited and we add more confusion to the future.

⊕ **Quote of the Day:** Every time you change your attitude, destiny is changed.

DAY 6

Real consciences efforts for truth help man to overcome obstacle and achieve his own good.

Consciousness is life's force and the soul's eyes. Following the path of yearnings, the truth of the self is found.

⊕ **Quote of the Day:** Remember not to live waiting for the world. The world is waiting for you.

DAY 7

When we understand the inscrutability of life, we understand mortality.

Understanding the whole, we evolve with the surroundings. We ponder the real and it's true distinctness, recognized that each matter has its own divine essence.

We raise awareness that life and its final goal is to create a collective harmony that will Transcend the senses.

⊕ **Quote of the Day:** Not all thoughts are based on understanding; some of them are capable of Blocking our vital energy and the divine as well.

DAY 8

Acting wisely is to accept the own years and not to mourn the younger years left behind.

Time is the accumulation of experiences, which give us strength, confidence, and pull us away from our own repressions (limitations). Each experience has its own clue and identity.

✦ **Quote of the Day:** Why stumble on someone else's stone if you know it hurts?

DAY 9

Questions about our existence and its intrinsic responses, make us realize the saying, "There will never will be absolute truth". Rather there are guides to discover the mysteries of being.

✦ **Quote of the Day:** Remember to live each day accepting your humanity, without denying yourself.

DAY 10

Not understanding the importance of the search for the inner truth, lets pity be born, a feeling that opens the door to low self-esteem. When we know and accept ourselves with confidence, the negative reaction and the wrong opinion of others, won't affect us.

✦ **Quote of the Day:** Do not forget that since the world has existed, there has always been opposition.

DAY 11

With at least two opinions, disagreement will exist.

Right reason will manifest at the moment when the ones involved accept that they alone do not Own the truth, that is to say, when the collective good is manifested, rather than individual ego.

✦ **Quote of the Day:** The Creator's will is unique and its teaching fits all and manifests for all. It is the intrinsic truth in the human essence, not in its reason.

DAY 12

Perpetual success is harmonious and well deserved. Success don't comes from a material process, instead it is the result of our daily inner essence actions; kindness, simplicity and love.

This is the way, to get a superior mark over the common men.

✦ **Quote of the Day:** Don't forget that the kind actions contribute to the meaning of life.

DAY 13

Experience will reveal our emotions and give us confidence.

Confidence pushes human actions beyond the limitations of thought, and the narrowness of intellect and wealth. Assurance is intrinsic to our mind; she unites us to the universal whole.

✦ **Quote of the Day:** If you want to express your experience with wisdom, you must accept it with honesty.

DAY 14

Reasonable man, accepts himself and his surroundings; living in constant understanding, in search of his soul's purpose.

✦ **Quote of the Day:** Knowledge can calm the mind and spirit; even if one has passed through pain to achieve it.

DAY 15

Purification is a process of constant healing, starting from the inside out.

The Compass is to focus on the experiences, emotions and harmonious interactions with the surroundings. There must be a balance between self and actions, but applying the knowledge and experiences processed, otherwise life is focused on a vicious cycle of ups and downs, plus emotional darkness.

✠ **Quote of the Day:** Understanding is a constant learning with some right guesses and some errors.

DAY 16

According to spirituality law, positive attracts positive.

Transformation is a synonym of change. Once we are on the way we shall be like a river's flow, placid, crystalline and pure. The starting point is not an obligation, it is necessity.

✠ **Quote of the Day:** Be yourself, but different than yesterday. Be a channel of peace.

DAY 17

Is the spiritual centered on all that in theory transcends all physical life?

Spiritual problems are just as visible and palpable as physical and material ones.

✠ **Quote of the Day:** These words are always associated in the spiritual realm: Difficulty Vis à Vis Existence, Certainty Vis à Vis Doubt, Pain Vis à Vis Destiny, Proceed Vis à Vis Conscience, and Discomfort Vis à Vis Miracle.

DAY 18

Says the popular adage: The calm comes after the storm.

We shouldn't decide to just leave painful circumstances behind, while crossing arms and accepting the bitterness with resignation, as we stick our head in the sand. We must learn to be better human beings in adversity and understand it not only with love, but also learn how to so live.

✦ **Quote of the Day:** With knowledge you can adjust to circumstances of life; either by changing them, applying or accepting them with harmony and responsibility.

DAY 19

Harmonious calm comes only from spiritual peace.

Peace with the Creator comes from the intrinsic essence of the self and of the religion we Profess. Is also divine energy, running freely. Responsibility to live in peace; is our strength.

✦ **Quote of the Day:** Walking peacefully is when you feel a peace even amidst the noise.

DAY 20

Man has rooted many aspects harmful to the soul through time, such as, sterile beliefs in the mental and spiritual centers.

The Compass is to eliminate the sterile aspects, beginning with understanding that the will of the Creator is absolute.

✦ **Quote of the Day:** The answer to all that has been written, spoken and discussed between the spiritual and religious is: "Love the Creator above all things", you are that creature.

DAY 21

Comparisons lead to weariness. We are unique, but equal beings; each one has a purpose to fulfill, but on the same path.

When we acquire honesty, we know our purpose as spiritual beings in all correlated to us, but in harmony. We meet the exact point of unifying our humanity with our divine essence.

✣ **Quote of the Day:** Our honesty is enhanced, when we confront the decisions of life with responsibility and confidence.

DAY 22

When we do not feel our emotions, in emotional limbo, what can we offer?

Like a dual energy flow, if the expression (emotion) is obstructed, you cannot feel.

Repression of emotions is our defense, against the fear of rejection.

✣ **Quote of the Day:** Expressing from the inside is the only way to know what you need to understand.

DAY 23

Plentitude of life begins with acceptance.

To accept ourselves just what we are lays the foundation of our integrity, and we are not afraid of ourselves.

✣ **Quote of the Day:** Avoid isolation if you want to experience the world in total harmony and believe in yourself, the good.

DAY 24

Repressions lead us to a life of addiction or situations that control us, affecting us physically and spiritually; the cause of our fear and pain.

✥ **Quote of the Day:** Before blaming others for the lack of peace around you, analyze first how much light is within you.

DAY 25

Dependency will not satisfy the needs of the soul, just the physical ones; our emotions become reduced, including our repression towards to those.

Being in charge of our emotions is to reach the essence of the self, and wisdom joins us in the act.

✥ **Quote of the Day:** A mind that is under control generates emotional peace and is fearless. There is no fear of change, but acceptance of experiences.

DAY 26

How do we know that we are in a right process of acceptance?

When we feel that emotions unleash within us and we don't understand the source of them.

The Compass is to focus on our experiences, with the desire to be better and grow; not to impose our will.

✥ **Quote of the Day:** Acceptance renews you and you live in peace with your surroundings.

DAY 27

Erroneous experiences from the past are not a punishment.

Generally experiences are a crucial part in the here and now of the harmonious life. They have the ability to limit or not our good deeds. Experiences help us resolve the daily concerns, according to our state of conscience.

⊕ **Quote of the Day:** You will be dwelling in the past when you do not accept your experiences.

DAY 28

Is human proceed to believe that we are invulnerable to pain; pain as an emotion benumbed state that surrounds us with loneliness and dissatisfaction. To seek or accept support is far from our mind; it wraps us in fear of expressing emotions and we anchor in an inner emptiness.

⊕ **Quote of the Day:** With light there is no emptiness and there is a reason to exist.

Day 29

We honor ourselves when we accept our divine energy.

Steps towards our honesty:

- Accept, understand, strengthen and harmonize experiences, feelings and emotions, in a single essence: Love.
- Moving from fear to certainty.
- Discarding afflictions.
- Keep a balance with what gives us peace.
- Never forget that life continues with its "Retroactive law".

⊕ **Quote of the Day:** More than a beautiful being you are divine, made to exist with glory and honor.

DAY 30

Wounds do not vanish by themselves; they will stay all the necessary time, till we accept our truth. They are painful experiences, with inner flows, which we don't want to process or accept. Denying them is like walking with closed eyes and the difference; the only difference, that the sixth sense will not rescue us.

⊕ **Quote of the Day:** Let flow or you will become a stagnant pod without depth, not clear placid water.

CHAPTER X

OCTOBER
IGNORANCE FLOWS FROM FOLLY

Smooth and real is the light in our eyes; when all is confusion and ignorance.

Unknown is the source of the wind and its goal; the same way we ignore the Creator's work.

There is a similarity between a darkened spiritual life and ignoring the truth. The fact that many of us live in comfort and joy, doesn't exempt us from folly and ignorance; where we forget to give, do well and sow good seeds.

It is ignorance to consider the fool a wise person, and honor him; because he lacks sanity in his actions.

A word of truth there is and it has been revealed to all; but even when it is heard and seen, it is still yet to be understood by all.

Whoever wants to hear, will hear, and whoever wants to see, will see. A wise person will not be disturbed by the mistakes of others, and understanding will free his soul.

In the darkness of ignorance is where we can get to reach the knowledge of light or vanish without even trying. The foul of ignorance, is torment to the soul. Lying due to ignorance limits inner growth.

DAY 1

Whoever lives in folly keeps his actions on its left side with his emotions.

The senseless one voices harmful words, acts by impulse, and always fails; he has no direction and lives with sloth as he gains an addict's strength.

Even in his thoughts, he speaks badly of others.

⊕ **Quote of the Day:** Life is more bearable with a strong spirit.

DAY 2

In terms of understanding, challenge and difficulty are not the same thing. Difficulties are a product of mental fallacies and fears. The challenge to our soul compels us to continue vibrantly in search of our own satisfaction, that is achieved when there is plentitude.

⊕ **Quote of the Day:** When we know ourselves, we accept challenges.

DAY 3

The uncertainties of daily life are without any doubt the foundation of our fear. Add to this our intrinsic weakness, for all time we spend without expression, and the ego.

A strong spirit is far from fear. Fear creates mental fallacies which lead us halfway across the bridge of life; but it is cut at both ends.

⊕ **Quote of the Day:** Behind fear truth too is hidden; doubts emerge!

DAY 4

When we do not accept ourselves, we create barriers that distance us from our divine attributes.

As we understand the meaning and purpose of experiences, we start a conscious integration with our "intrinsic essence", the soul and we acquire knowledge of what has already been there.

⊕ **Quote of the Day:** The answers are within the self; the ability to decry and complete your life's purpose, your destiny.

DAY 5

Emotions cannot be eliminated from the soul's memory; they are positive and harmonious.

Feelings can be negative, and they cannot be replaced by other positive actions or attitude.

Negative feelings can only be removed by cutting the source at the root; the essence that causes them to exist.

⊕ **Quote of the Day:** Your emotions are the manifestation of the soul, and they manifest to harmonize with the whole.

DAY 6

Life is a process, not a result. We are, in this world of matter and substance, a spiritual essence, and we must adjust to experiences if we want to achieve harmonious learning and emotional growth.

Knowledge, without doubt, keeps us in control against a world of material and sensorial temptation.

⊕ **Quote of the Day:** Keep focused on the daily learning with conscience, if you want to clarify your spiritual purpose and cope with the ups and downs of daily life.

DAY 7

When we are involved with our personal growth, we come into harmony with the surroundings; where each trial is part of the evolving process.

When there is no blame towards anyone or anything, no dissatisfaction, something within us is in evolutionary acceptance; getting better with conscience.

⊕ **Quote of the Day:** Understanding is part of living in harmony within the whole universe.

DAY 8

Daily life gets converted into a routine when we act without awareness.

To get away from routine, we must fill our lives with purpose and challenges; these changes must be positive, progressive and consistent. We must not distance ourselves from our imagination; since she is the best ally to see the yearnings come true.

⊕ **Quote of the Day:** Miracles can manifest even during the most insignificant moments.

DAY 9

On the way to the understanding, never is there an end; there is always something new to learn.

Ignorance is so unpredictable, that starting the path with it, we never know what ends first, the path or the ignorant one.

✦ **Quote of the Day:** The evolution of understanding even and ever end.

DAY 10

An unexpressed yearning has its roots truncated; due to the fact that its motivations and essence are not in harmony (free expression).

Yearnings are part of our earthly purpose, as a being of light in constant evolution; not like a irrational being with incomplete and confusing perceptions.

✦ **Quote of the Day:** You must be aware of the role that your ego or your divine essence are playing in your yearnings.

DAY 11

When we are unable to perceive the harmonious flow of our emotions; we will not recognize, much less express them. Emotions, even when contradictory, are intrinsically related to reason and intellect; therefore they are part of inner self-growth.

✦ **Quote of the Day:** Ignorance fuels the manifestation of our limitations.

DAY 12

With knowledge there is interaction between the psychic and the spiritual; therefore not everything that is real is true. True knowledge is the one which connects us to our consciousness; causes us to evolve.

⊕ **Quote of the Day:** Following a true reason is the only way to salvation.

DAY 13

The destiny of an unconscious man falls into two paths; leaves things to random or takes action. Random helps us ease our life and to accept joy or frustration, where our destiny is limited. With reasonable action we combat the random adversity, and we search for a fruitful destiny, where reality doesn't confound us.

⊕ **Quote of the Day:** Where you focus your energy on, becomes part of your destiny.

DAY 14

We must not turn back when we advance.

The physical body is the one who walks and returns; the spirit always moves forward in a constant state of rotation and change.

What is knowledge good for if you do not move into action? Action lays the ground for the greatness of wisdom.

⊕ **Quote of the Day:** Any new change is a satisfaction but not a design.

DAY 15

Spiritual work has unlimited connection with challenges.

There is always something new to handle and experience. Many things are explained as they are experienced; accepted knowledge makes them bearable.

⊕ **Quote of the Day:** Your world's extension will be measured with the knowledge's ruler.

DAY 16

What make us think that miracles are not attached to the truth?

Assurance becomes a miracle when the same is an attempt by our physical nature for its realization.

⊕ **Quote of the Day:** Truth exists because of creation and reaches it.

DAY 17

Spirituality may silence us, as it makes us observers and willing to listen.

As we listen our environment we learn about its essence. The Compass is dedicated attention, if we want to express with good perception.

⊕ **Quote of the Day:** If you want to be heard, speak as if you are the one who listens.

DAY 18

A calm spirit is like an antidote to a troubled soul.

If the time sequence is destroyed, the evolutionary process of the self comes to a stop.

The sequence to overcome mistakes and develop virtues, to acquire a deep knowledge about existence.

⊕ **Quote of the Day:** A problem solved is a gifted won.

DAY 19

The highest perfection of the self is the plentitude of life.

We reach plentitude when we open our minds to understanding man has trouble understanding the world, due to his lack of conscience.

✦ **Quote of the Day:** A man in harmony doesn't suffer, and he doesn't cause martyrdom.

DAY 20

Even to spend time in search of understanding, we need to be a connoisseur.

Life will always go on; even when we are unaware about the path to take.

Idleness is a dangerous perfection, is a perfection of nothing and a death foretold.

✦ **Quote of the Day:** The wise prefer the impossible, because the possible is already done.

DAY 21

The power of knowledge is so influential it makes birds talk and animals dance. Even so, men are devoid of reason. The absence of knowledge will cause a trial.

✦ **Quote of the Day:** Education makes the man and spirituality strengthens his soul.

DAY 22

One of ignorance's common mistakes is to leave the future aside; falling into a fallacy that there is nothing else to learn.

Not being as great as we wish this time of life, is no reason to be less good and eloquent than we can be.

✦ **Quote of the Day:** If you don't want to get frustrated, don't have expectations. You must act!

DAY 23

The one who does not admit a warning, much less will accept advice.

Intolerance is a reflection of our own discontent and inner unrest.

✦ **Quote of the Day:** There is no lost reason but the one you don't want to understand.

DAY 24

Past experiences tie our responsibility with the present and the hope for the future; for that the experiences must be accepted. We build our yearnings based on them, helping us to understand that the sense of life is timely, placid and liberating.

✦ **Quote of the Day:** Past limitations, if justified, become present defeat and existential frustration in the future.

DAY 25

You can change the way you talk, even your language; but you will always express what you carry on the inside.

The level of humility and morality is measured according to our knowledge of the truth.

✦ **Quote of the Day:** Try not to fall prey to insults and search for the true, if you want to have a peaceful life.

DAY 26

Pride is the best way to be ridiculous.

Humility cannot be assumed to be an obligation, nor a condition. Humility simply arises and stays where the ego doesn't win.

⊕ **Quote of the Day:** Ignorance and pride go hand by hand.

DAY 27

Thought precedes the will, it can be the origin of an action or its frustration.

The impetuous action of the ego enslaves. Our freedom manifests when we are able to keep the ego under control with our thoughts. Without freedom, man will not be able to fulfill his destiny.

⊕ **Quote of the Day:** True freedom doesn't need to be exhibit, (debauchery) but feel it (plentitude). Freedom is a natural manifestation of the being.

DAY 28

There is nothing wrong with a state of poverty, except when it is mixed with laziness; while we become arrogant, ignorant and vulgar.

The argument of a senseless man who is also proud, is at the same level of the intelligent one without justice, both nulls.

⊕ **Quote of the Day:** Truth is like the daylight; be careful if while being on front of it, you are looking for a lamp.

DAY 29

What about those who consider themselves being alive?

Inert beings, absurd; hiding behind the ego of their ignorance; prevailing darkness.

Pitiful life in the shadows, within the echo of suffering; frivolity remains because of lack of understanding.

✦ **Quote of the Day:** Happiness becomes stronger as man is able to overcome his bewilderment.

DAY 30

Light, as a source of energy, is perceived through the emotions, physical light manifests through the senses.

The light is interpreted by the senses as a harmonious energy of our being. It happens the same way with our autonomous capacity of understanding, and also with the absolute control of our DNA. Understandings depends on the intensity of light in our essence.

✦ **Quote of the Day:** We were created to reason, find and understand, not to react, forget and ignore.

DAY 31

Is a life trivial? Unfortunate events will unfold without any notice.

When following a path of light and truth, there is no damage after failure.

We are so big and perfect that we can initiate change from within; without needing others to do it.

✦ **Quote of the Day:** Opportunities do not come alone; they also bring errors.

CHAPTER XI

NOVEMBER
CHARITY PRECEDES JUSTICE

Human justice is not the Achilles Heel of creation; as long as its foundation is rooted in divine justice's fear.

Where there is a just person, there is also: justice, truth, equality, respect, consideration, affection, emotions, love and peace. With Peace, there is everything and as all things endure there is life not destruction, and where life is, the Creator dwells.

Regarding ignorance and justice there is oversight. Wisdom will always put us in the right, with no hesitation, bias, irrational passion or injustice.

We must discipline ourselves in time, before others do it for us; before reason tells us it too late.

Are you ready for the Olympics of Justice? Here are the first contest to enter; experiences:

- Ego, selfishness and envy vs. light.
- Love, yearning and support vs. darkness.

Feelings and emotions are the cause of our actualization. It is with them that we can or can't make right our actions, our lives.

DAY 1

People who seem to us unimportant or unknown, have a lesson to teach us; if we want to arrive at our destination, "so that we may know ourselves".

The daily routine of looking in the mirror does not guarantee that we will accept ourselves just as we are.

The ego inheres in human nature and as such it makes us feel perfect; whereas in fact we are not. We have the ability to accept us and to change for better.

✠ **Quote of the Day:** Humility is synonymous with wisdom, and is the best antidote to Ego.

DAY 2

We are all stars that shine with our own light.

There is no need to be the biggest star, but to be able to give the best from our interior.

The action of giving must not be that simply; but to have conscience in it. It is better to give than receive.

✠ **Quote of the Day:** Sharing is also an expression of the soul.

DAY 3

Why surrender to the undeserving crowd, as the world has a plenty of space, and if at the end of the storm the sky is always blue?

Wait and beware of the times and the nonsense, so that stumbling and deceit do not take you by surprise.

⊕ **Quote of the Day:** There are no bad moments, only different opportunities.

DAY 4

To understand our psychological truth, we must eliminate our harmful characteristics.

The negative aspects of the self must be separated from our essence in order to achieve plentitude.

The more we hide our vulnerability, the more we become fragile and intolerant. Weaknesses like the ego grow faster than humility, and our spirituality sublimity.

⊕ **Quote of the Day:** Where there is a challenge, there is light. The most important and transcendental about the challenge is not to recognize it, nor to accept it but finish it.

DAY 5

Let us not be anxious over yesterday, today or tomorrow's problems; they are part of our perfection and they will disappear when we depart.

The road to success is like the fight against sleep; when we are unaware, it catches us by surprise, and then we wake up feeling better than ever.

⊕ **Quote of the Day:** To overcome the problem's fears, we must be brave.

DAY 6

Happiness is an attribute of the brave and a fruit of his harmony.

A frustrating job can become a favorite habit, when we assume that want it.

✦ **Quote of the Day:** To develop your gift, you need talent as well.

DAY 7

The expression "step into another person's shoes", is a popular riddle that tells of walking the other person's life, feeling and understanding the source of the emotions, joy and pain that befall the person; comprehending, we get the ability to help.

There is no need to be an intellectual to accept this approach; just to be fair and sage, having morality and honesty.

✦ **Quote of the Day:** Giving is better than receiving. One needs to be in harmony with one's emotions and one's surroundings in order to recognize the need to help.

DAY 8

When you feel that life is hard to comprehend; is because we are spiritual dwarves. This faulty perception is created by a state of unconsciousness and fear.

We must focus on defeating the ego, as it makes us walk away from gratitude, kindness, justice and tolerance. The ego is a barrier to plentitude and appreciation of who we really are.

✦ **Quote of the Day:** Do not lose enthusiasm and do not stop fighting for your yearnings, no matter how small they are.

DAY 9

Ingratitude tends to darken and shrivel emotions; it pulls us away from goodness and justice. Ingratitude opens a gap on the spiritual path; it is like growing without deep roots so that sooner or later we will fall, unable to help ourselves or others.

✦ **Quote of the Day:** Our thoughts and actions reveal the truth of our emotions.

DAY 10

The harmonious essence of the soul is what fills our existence with passion to live; otherwise we live in gloomy darkness with a lasting existential nightmare.

The harmonious soul gives its all; in this irrational world of fallacies and vanities. We are intolerance, even of our own needs. Having our eyes open doesn't mean we are awake.

✦ **Quote of the Day:** You are beginning your spiritual purpose, when you decide to walk away from yourself.

DAY 11

Correcting ourselves will help us appreciate the qualities of others.

We believe to be in the plentitude in our lives, when we feel greatest.

What is greatness? Plentitude, comes when we are "brave"; is a state of conscious strength that eliminates weakness. Greatness, as a feeling, is a fallacy of conscious weakness.

Living in plentitude, is to break free of limitations, learning to share, to act with no selfishness. When we annul the ego, ignore envy, living in gratitude, acting with kindness we learn to evolve with what we have.

✦ **Quote of the Day:** Greatness is full of deserved honors and gratuitous pardons as well.

DAY 12

Temporary luck is for the deluded; lasting success is for the wise.

In the quest for true knowledge, we cannot settle for the first thing that appears in front us; what it is ready at hand for everyone is just the mediocre and ordinary.

There is no unanswerable question and no fact without its truth; we just have to be vigilant so we do not fall into the lasting error of a dead routine.

✦ **Quote of the Day:** In order to understand, we need to know how to ask.

DAY 13

Ever slipped a pebble in your shoe?

Words are symbols when not pronounced, intolerant when they hurt the consciousness, fleeting when we do not understand them, liberating when they are true. They are cruel when they are clothed with injustice, and they are the all in an empty world if they are filled with love.

Words can also become nothing more than a simple pebble; frivolous, irregular, inert, almost eternal and indestructible: Such word-pebbles unresolved become stumbling blocks in the path of confusion and doubt.

✦ **Quote of the Day:** Do not let that pebble stay in your shoe.

DAY 14

Fear of accepting our responsibilities leads to a state of unconsciousness guilt, which destroys our self-esteem, a loss of human values, and a lack of love.

We are not here to judge and dictate to others how to live. We most know how to honor ourselves and how to respect the intrinsic beauty of others.

✥ **Quote of the Day:** The sage man accepts himself and his surroundings; living in constant movement, in search of his soul purpose.

DAY 15

A spiritual fall has more pain, sorrow and confusion than a physical fall.

Standing on our feet takes away the scandal of others; spiritual standing releases us from inner shame. This action releases us and does not limit our self-esteem.

✥ **Quote of the Day:** When you overcome grief, you gain blessing.

DAY 16

Urges generated from the ego are inane and bring limitations.

Humility is a manifestation of the soul, the ego is a human manifestation that causes weakness.

Humility fights for spirituality; the ego is like a glooming darkness, humility is like a bright glow in the darkness. The ego is like a false glimmer, while humility is the truth that enlightens the soul.

✥ **Quote of the Day:** Deliverance from the ego means urges are not what they used to be.

DAY 17

Do not ignore the feeling of emptiness within.

Feeling safe is the result of being able to perceive our emotions. It provides an existential aptitude that will lead us to a personal encounter.

A conscious knowledge will not take us away from the human essence and the purpose, destiny.

✦ **Quote of the Day:** Emptiness and its manifestations will not replace what is already empty.

DAY 18

Do not reject your parents, but rather honor them. When you reject your parents, you reject yourself; if you honor them, you evolve. Do not embark following their mistakes; rather you evolve with them, so you can find joy and life's meaning. Benign feelings will supply more than we can need.

✦ **Quote of the Day:** To err is equally wrong as trying to justify it.

DAY 19

Negative facts and circumstances have a positive aspect that looks contradictory, but as we accept them we improve our knowledge and spirit. Not everything that looks quiet remains still and well. We enhance our self-essence as we fly against the wind; not when we glide on the winds of sophistry.

✦ **Quote of the Day:** Anything that was created out of nothingness is of invaluable price.

DAY 20

Gifts and talents are of divine privilege, we must assume them responsibly. Take them with peaceful guile and good sense. Success, with merit, will be achieved when we get rid of egocentric traits. Talents help us transcend our individuality, due to the fact that we are collective beings.

⊕ **Quote of the Day:** Strive to be original if you want your actions to be commended.

DAY 21

It is in the silence of words where we hear the whispers of the soul; then we perceive the real sound around us and perception departs from the senses.

The absence of thought and stillness of the body activates freedom of the spirit. Everything that is captured in this level of consciousness changes us for the better.

⊕ **Quote of the Day:** When you are confident and know how to wait in silence, everything in your surroundings will assist you.

DAY 22

Woe to those who sell their liberty for a sophistry of vain happiness.

Liberty is measured according to the ruling of urges. When the material prevails against our harmony, we become servants of wealth; entering such a state where we have to do, rather than be.

⊕ **Quote of the Day:** Your riches are the ones that you do not change even for all the gold in the world.

DAY 23

Our ideals and aspirations in our future, make the pitfalls of the present bearable.

Frustrations and suffering arise when the unequivocal reason of man gives value to the meaningless; refusing to understand the fundamentals aspects to a harmonious existence.

✥ **Quote of the Day:** We must know and understand the true value of our surroundings in order to know the meaning of life.

DAY 24

Fears are intrinsic to men, the same as mortality; with the difference that fears have solution.

Calling into question what we believe is our reason, we shall not fear the solitude, if we walk on plentitude path; it is there where the self finds its freedom.

✥ **Quote of the Day:** Unhappiness brings misery and existential slavery.

DAY 25

Opportunities may or not be unique; what is true is that they are not the same, if they came back. We do not leave things for tomorrow, unless it is something that never shall be done, ever.

✥ **Quote of the Day:** Limitations are traced by you; yearning with conscience and change your tactics.

DAY 26

Individualism shall not be confused with individuality.

Individualism is based on what you have. Individuality is based on what one is; no matter how big or small our possessions are.

The most improbable of our reason, is the one which portrays an empty life; the one that we try to create without a margin of error, but at the end brings the deceit of the imperturbable.

⊕ **Quote of the Day:** Plentitude is the absolute peace of having it all, but without having it. How plenty are you?

DAY 27

The past is the best allied within the whole.

It may sound paradoxical, but past helps us grow when we cope with it. There is no doubt the past can destroy us when we rebel against it, and fall into confusion. Injustice drags us, and we blame others for our senseless.

⊕ **Quote of the Day:** All returns as a result of a past action.

DAY 28

Silence and solitude have an important meaning; they nourish the true personal encounter.

Silence's power proceeds the storm and emerges after it and can our reason but make us perceive the mystical notes of what surrounds us.

Silence is a strange calm that thrills us and puts an end to larger exaltations, offenses and injustices.

⊕ **Quote of the Day:** Happiness in solitude, is a unique emotional state of those who do not fear themselves.

DAY 29

Someone's prosperity, is simply the opportunity that an innocuous man allowed to pass.

The future has a world of possibilities we cannot anticipate; but witch, with the knowledge of our destiny, we overcome.

Opportunities, even with challenge, are and will be a step forward to the future, never to the past.

⊕ **Quote of the Day:** The best card will not help, if you do not know how to play.

DAY 30

Listening is a gift, just as important as the spoken word; the absence of both gives way to the fallacy of judging.

A wise man doesn't criticize other people's errors, rather joins them while showing a higher truth. Never use admonition, but kindness.

Quote of the Day: Unlike the adage "Silence gives consent"; the silence of the wise is also wise.

CHAPTER XII

DECEMBER
WE ARE LOVE

Love, feeling that appears in the human being as energy that transforms everything to positive, it is the ultimate expression of the positive energy of the human being, and manifests through the senses, mind and touch.

Love doesn't come from the instincts; if such were the case, we would be living without compassion, without remorse, without pain, and with bitterness. Love is the ability to give, help, forgive and understand.

Is love then a genetic gift, or it is conditional to a cultural, religious, social or familial pattern and particular experiences?

The meaning of love and the self is complex due to the unexpected reactions of the human mind and behavior.

We are like a blank paper, when we born, inexperienced, ignorant of the meaning of our feelings, and much less our emotions.

Receiving a pattern conditioned by the surroundings, our aptitude and attitude are a reflection of the learned and observed. This may influence the ability to love. It may or may not be born.

If there is lack of love, there may not love to give. Love is able to open doors to the inner light, for the giver and the receiver.

Received in the genetic patterns it is inactive, but ready to be born at any time, only needing inspiration and momentum to flourish, and then its capacity will be endless.

Love is the primary essence of the universe and life; it is the source of emotions, having in it no room for dark influences.

DAY 1

Beauty needs to be perceived in order to be found.

Appreciating life's beauty is part of the love-emotion, is the intrinsic nature of the self.

The Compass is to focus on the present and all the harmonious in our lives.

⊕ **Quote of the Day:** What we see is appreciated according as we are.

DAY 2

Do not search too far nor wait long, for what? Everything is within you!

Spirituality and intellectuality run parallel paths along the way; the combination of them plus conscience state, make us wise and with plenitude in from others; we all have the ability to be thus endowed.

⊕ **Quote of the Day:** The truth will be your own light.

DAY 3

There is no love without conscience.

Life is full of sheer joy, when we understand that we are part of a universal whole, and our essence unites us, one and all

✦ **Quote of the Day:** Having appreciation for the environment gives us love's joy.

DAY 4

Unconditional love is the one that exceeds moments of pain that others cause us; not the one that only comes when others satisfy us. Love, just as time, heals all wounds even though the scars and memories remain.

✦ **Quote of the Day:** The only important thing is how we are given love and how we love.

DAY 5

Feelings cannot be avoided, but can be controlled.

Pain cannot be avoided without pain, love cannot be felt without love; sharing cannot be happen without recognizing needs, doubt cannot be denied inside of confusion, and thoughts cannot be expressed without reflect our inner selves.

Observing the surroundings with our emotions perceive and dazzle with the truth

✦ **Quote of the Day:** Darkness exists in the senses, not in the emotions.

DAY 6

Love in all its manifestations is the divine flow of energy within our emotions.

The ability to love, helps us comprehend, understand and accept the existence of the Creator and his cosmic manifestation.

✦ **Quote of the Day:** It is the origin and master of the world. Without love, all would be nothingness.

DAY 7

Love is light, hatred is darkness. Love and hatred are related antonyms. One cannot hate when one has loved; but one can love, when there has been hate; there is adage, "There is one step from hatred to love".

✦ **Quote of the Day:** Absence of truth is lack of love.

DAY 8

Solely the wise have assurance. They know how grasp and when to let go, when blend with the surroundings or be apart to achieve a spiritual harmony. The prudent learn to use loneliness as a renewal in the process of achieving plentitude.

✦ **Quote of the Day:** Do not use loneliness as a solace for your misfortune.

DAY 9

Love is a small word, but so big that it means everything.

A grateful attitude towards life enables an energy, makes to flow individual and collective blessings flow.

Love and wisdom make the truth blossom, and are the best way to sustain our existence.

✦ **Quote of the Day:** Love is the strength to live without fear or limitations.

DAY 10

Where there is love, there is also compassion.

Charity, like mercy, is the daily fare of the soul.

Love blooms when we are walking on in search of our spiritual plentitude.

⊕ **Quote of the Day:** Do not judge, love!

DAY 11

The journey to know and enjoy life involves simplicity, responsibility and determination; we shall not carry the burdens of ingratitude, laziness, and ignorance.

⊕ **Quote of the Day:** Love is the beginning of responsibilities.

DAY 12

How to be aware of whom we love?

Man is prone to imitate those he loves; therefore his ability to love governs his own plentitude level.

⊕ **Quote of the Day:** Watching others, you know what they love and how much they have forgiven.

DAY 13

Why? Is a question mark, intrinsic of man; the effect would be different if, instead of using it as a complaint seeking denial, we used it to search for plentitude.

The "why" related to complaining represents lack, while the "why" related to appropriation carries gratitude.

✦ **Quote of the Day:** Giving thanks brings plenitude, gives you comfort and feeds the self-esteem, thus makes the gift of love flow; blessings.

DAY 14

Rest is not a synonym of peace, peace is a harmony between the physical body and the spirit. Peace is not the contrary of war; rather it is a state of emotion that harmonizes us with the environment. Lack of harmony is what leads to conflicts and war.

✦ **Quote of the Day:** Tolerance and love for all, are the foundations of inner peace.

DAY 15

The language of passion is easier to learn and the vainest to express; very different from the language of love. Love in couples is like applause, it needs two halves to manifest.

✦ **Quote of the Day:** Open eyes are not enough to see the true love that others offer you.

DAY 16

Perfection is in us!

We have to understand with certainty and strength to achieve the impossible. We must cope our truth, even if it is uncomfortable and accept that everyone is perfect as they are.

✦ **Quote of the Day:** According to your degree of harmony, truth, unlike a lie, will always make you well.

DAY 17

The goal is here, on every evolutionary level, where all is possible with sharing and loving.

Love has the ability to save, enhance and redeem, moreover, given the will to make others happy.

✥ **Quote of the Day:** Change your conscience, living in harmony with your soul.

DAY 18

Humility is a manifestation of the soul, while the ego is a human manifestation.

Where there is humility we love, where there is ego we idolize ourselves.

Ego is the defense of our human weakness, humility is the struggle of our spirituality.

Ego is glooming darkness, while humility is light in the darkness.

The ego is a hallucinatory lie; humility is truth that lightens our soul.

✥ **Quote of the Day:** Humility is another way to connect with the Creator.

DAY 19

Inner change is more compelling than outer change; the latter is the focus of envy; while interior change brings love. Love is frees and envy limits.

⊕ **Quote of the Day:** What kind of change are you willing to make?

DAY 20

Love is unpredictable, there is no manual explaining its manifestations, or even how to experience one's mistakes.

We must know how to wait for it and make it our plentitude; because we don't know where it is, how and when we will find it and when it will end.

⊕ **Quote of the Day:** Loving and forgiving give you happiness; are the basic first steps toward your plenitude.

DAY 21

Yielding means winning. It is a synonym of kindness.

Love is compassion, justice is human; love elevates and justice sets limits.

The power of love neutralizes mishaps of the mind, allowing us harmonious manifestations.

⊕ **Quote of the Day:** Kindness is a true love manifestation of the Soul.

DAY 22

Love as expression of the senses; but in combination with the divine essence and our conscience, it will be manifest without equivocation or limit. Otherwise, it is only passion; a unilateral expression of the senses.

Love is a physical plentitude, emotional; as such, it transcends the senses and is an unconditional manifestation.

✣ **Quote of the Day:** Supposed love comes from the ego. Emptiness results and will persist.

DAY 23

There is no mistake in the Creator's will.

If there is no yearning from the soul, you will be not heard; the same happens to our need for spiritual sublimity.

What is meant to be will be, no matter how severe it seems, it will be.

The conversation with the Creator, will express his will, and the initiative of the soul.

✣ **Quote of the Day:** Ego is not a best ally to get away from suffering.

DAY 24

Understanding we are more spiritual than physical beings, we connect with love's essence; which it is as essential to life, as breathing.

We are the ones responsible for its manifestation, not depending on others.

✣ **Quote of the Day:** Knowing yourself is an art learned in the school of silence; leading you to become a master of spirituality.

DAY 25

Spiritual laziness may lead us to clone negative traits of others.

The Compass is in assuming these reflections, looking to deploy our essence; since we are spiritual beings, unique souls.

✦ **Quote of the Day:** Spirituality is living daily with common sense; discipline will make you grow in gratitude and love.

DAY 26

You can be successful in many aspects of life; but harmony with the surroundings is what gives you perpetuity.

Success is a combination of yearning and need. Longing lead us to great achievements, needs are a reality of daily living. They are not essential to our existence and they can be replaced.

Longing goes beyond needs, which are individual in their existence.

✦ **Quote of the Day:** Irrational need will remain, as it is never satiated. Longing transforms itself, following a constant course in the perpetual evolution of each being.

DAY 27

Sometimes we fail our mission and we feel deceived, so we say "This karma!" At some point we think that what happened is a misfortune not to us; but to those around us, who didn't deserve that privilege after our blessings.

✦ **Quote of the Day:** The only lives lost, are those that do not want to try again.

DAY 28

Stubbornness as popularly called, is no more than a mistaken and egocentric manifestation.

Ego is a dark manifestation of the emotions and the root of human baseness. It is a psychological patron with the evil power to affect the self, attacking hope and not letting love emerge.

⊕ **Quote of the Day:** Do not confuse ego with perseverance.

DAY 29

Love is perceived differently; to some it is sanity and madness to others.

Love is part of our divine essence and is permanent; its foundation is compassion and understanding.

Our ability to love is a reflection of the "I", our intrinsic value.

⊕ **Quote of the Day:** You decide your own value and how much you are willing to love.

DAY 30

Regrets about the past give us a present filled with guilt and a future full of fears.

The Compass is to let the light shine over what is forgotten, understanding that clinging to pain and guilt brings a sad future and doubt; making us slaves to ourselves and causing fear to change.

⊕ **Quote of the Day:** Those who don't admit theirs errors are equally cowardly as those who silently hide the truth.

DAY 31

The soul's biggest shame is to turn your back on the person who it loves.

Learning to live, not just to love, is accepting challenges and errors.

Honoring life is the best way to enjoy it. We must move away from the vanity and its fallacy, which leads us to a world of errors.

A life of freedom, like the good love, doesn't depend of coincidences and much less is it imposed.

✦ **Quote of the Day:** Love attracts more love!

SYNOPSIS

Your eternal compass is to be in plentitude during your journey, without forgetting the already traveled, your experiences.

There will always be a better way to go; reconstruct yourself with bravery. How? Change your attitude for the better, harmonize with your inner self and look within yourself for goodness; your power.

When you reconsider your attitude, you get away from incomprehensible disorders. The glow of light begins guiding your steps to new ways of understanding, and onward to prolonged success. Understanding will bring your inner peace, which will be projected onto your surroundings. Anger is the result of repressed feelings and experiences, which lead to constant frustration, pushing us towards to pain; with its facets of anxiety, depression and panic. There is refusal to accept, give and Love. Hostility kills the spirit, makes you age without living.

Do not forget, your soul needs you; activate your inner self and your finite mind. It is now that your inner self is calling you to follow a true path of wisdom and mercy which will give you the power to pursue; the Light.

~There are no words you cannot understand; neither are there eternal secrets that cannot become your truth; there is no darkness without light or an intricate labyrinth.

The essence of existence is within you; regardless of your chosen path, do not forget to put in your purse "The Compass to your plentitude". ~

Maropeta

BIOGRAPHY

A Colombian poet and writer at heart. Margarita is devoted to literature, and writing mystical reflections in metaphor and prose. Her writing style of mysticism and spirituality are found in her poems and stories, and describes the author as a vanguard writer.

She is a successful self-published author that also has International involvement in a collaboration of anthologies.

In her dedication to the arts, Margarita's accomplishments as an aspiring poet, active author and artist, had driven her to establish a cultural and international event in 2013: AZ LIBRIS SHOW. Her community involvement in the literary arts scene inspired this heartfelt effort to promote minority writers and artists in all expressions. This platform was created for those who generally have no structured support or resources to promote their talent and passion for the art.

The goal is to introduce local, national and International artists. The main focus is to assist and promote minority artists who may otherwise have no opportunity to participate in this growing industry through participation in eclectic artistic presentations in a wide range of mediums, poetry reciting's, literary excerpts, professional lecturers, and performing artists of music and of theatre.

Published Books:

Palabras... ¿Espejo de un Recuerdo? (Words... Mirror of a Memory?). Consists of a series of reflections on poetry for the soul and life. Filled pages of sensitivity, requiring a personal encounter. The book was nominated to Best E-Book Category Poetry - 2012 by Dan Poynter's Global E-Book. Awarded by AIPEH-Orlando with the Gold Medal for the contribution to Spanish literature. 2012.

Compas en la Existencia -Pasos a la Plenitud- (Compass in Existence - Steps to Wholeness -). Mystical and spiritual reflections that help transcend the barriers between the material and the spiritual stages, in the daily life of every person, yearnings for full understanding and peace. Medal of Honor in Spiritual category, not fiction. Awarded by Dan Poynter's Global E-Book 2014.

Awarded by AIPEH-Orlando with the Gold Medal for his contribution to Spanish literature. 2014.

Published Anthologies:

* Thousand poems to Cesar Vallejo. 2012. Peru. Participants Poems: Maybe view, Breezes... Years and Acrostic (Cesar Abraham Vallejo Mendoza).
* Thousand poems to Miguel Hernández. 2012. Peru. Participants Poems: Between Bars and What Poet or Martyr?
* Literary Work by SPE. Narrative-Short Story: Teaching Grandpa-2012 and Nova-2014.
* ELILUC Antologies: Poems participants: My other life-2012, Ancestral Pact- 2014 and Paradox-2015.
* Poets and Storytellers 2012- ICP. Participants Poems: interior Sea, Her lament, My Window, Day by Day, and The Poet's Anguish. Miami, 2012.

Events:

* International Miami Book Fair in November 2011 through 2015.
* Presentation of his works, to "Society of Poets and Writers of Miami", FL. 2012-2014.
* Literary Event: Friday of Literature at Colombia Embassy in Miami, FL. 2012.
* Literary Event: Book festival in Coral Gables, Florida, 2012.
* Presentation of his works at "AIPEH" International Association of Hispanic Culture Art. Orlando, FL. 2012-2014.
* Literary Event: Exhibition of arts and the book - ArtSpoken performing center. Miami, FL. 2012-2014.
* Friday Cultural "Calle Ocho" Literary event by ELILUC 2012-2014.
* Literary Event: ELILUC. Miami, FL. 2011 through 2015.
* Participation in the Miami Poetry Festival. Poems: Viernes y 33189, (Zip-Ode) chosen among the best. 2013-2015.
* Spanish Book Fair, West Palm Beach, FL. 2013-2014.
* Book Expo America, "New Titles Showcase" New York, NY. 2013.
* AZ LIBRIS SHOW, Miami, FL. 2013 through 2015.
* UCF Book Festival. "Central University of Florida." Orlando, FL. 2014.
* Nominated for Best Poetess, NPE Award- Night of Erotic Poetry. By ArtSpoken preform Center. Miami 2013, 2014 (Winner) and 2015 (Winner).
* Presentations at the Public Libraries of Hialeah and Homestead. 2013-2014.
* Private Presentations at FIU - Barnes & Noble store (Florida International University). 2015.

BIOGRAPHY

Contact:

Email: palabrasmw@aol.com

Twitter: @MargaritPedrozo

Linkedin: Margarita rosa pedrozo walling

Pinterest.com/maropeta

www.MargaritaRosaPedrozo-Walling.com

Facebook Official/page: Margarita Rosa Pedrozo Taboada

AZ LIBRIS SHOW: Facebook.com/AzLibrisShow

www.AZLIBRISSHOW.org

CPSIA information can be obtained at www.ICGtesting.com
Printed in the USA
BVOW08s2241290616

454022BV00001B/8/P